Building Bonds WITH *Learners*

The **Teacher-Student Relationship** Model

PATRICIA ERBE

Solution Tree | Press

555 North Morton Street
Bloomington, IN 47404
800.733.6786 (toll free) / 812.336.7700
FAX: 812.336.7790

email: info@SolutionTree.com
SolutionTree.com

Printed in the United States of America

Library of Congress Cataloging-in-Publication Data

Names: Erbe, Patricia, author.
Title: Building bonds with learners : the teacher-student relationship model / Patricia Erbe.
Description: Bloomington, IN : Solution Tree Press, 2024. | Includes bibliographical references and index.
Identifiers: LCCN 2024003807 (print) | LCCN 2024003808 (ebook) | ISBN 9781960574169 (paperback) | ISBN 9781960574176 (ebook)
Subjects: LCSH: Teacher-student relationships.
Classification: LCC LB1033 .E74 2024 (print) | LCC LB1033 (ebook) | DDC 371.102/3--dc23/eng/20240212
LC record available at https://lccn.loc.gov/2024003807
LC ebook record available at https://lccn.loc.gov/2024003808

Solution Tree
Jeffrey C. Jones, CEO
Edmund M. Ackerman, President

Solution Tree Press
President and Publisher: Douglas M. Rife
Associate Publishers: Todd Brakke and Kendra Slayton
Editorial Director: Laurel Hecker
Art Director: Rian Anderson
Copy Chief: Jessi Finn
Production Editor: Gabriella Jones-Monserrate
Proofreader: Evie Madsen
Content Development Specialist: Amy Rubenstein
Cover Designer: Abigail Bowen
Text Designer: Laura Cox
Associate Editor: Sarah Ludwig
Editorial Assistant: Anne Marie Watkins

Acknowledgments

About halfway into writing this book, I questioned Dr. Rhonda Rabbitt, dean of education at Wilkes University at the time, about the importance of this project and whether I should continue. After explaining its premise, she said, "There's a segment of teachers out there who need to hear your words." I am eternally grateful for her inspirational statement and the unconditional positivity she gave me along the way.

Others who supported me included my family and friends. You know who you are, and you were incredibly patient with me when I wrote for long hours and was sometimes unavailable. Thank you for tolerating me with my grand visions. I felt your love and support.

Thank you to Jane, a huge cheerleader for me, and Sharon, the fuel that kept me on track.

I would be remiss if I did not shout out to colleagues, students, and acquaintances willing to share their expertise or stories. Special thanks to the teacher panel: Julia DeAngelis, Meghan Stolnis, Carol DeMarco, Stefanie Dougherty, Jenny Khabursky, Megan Schell, and Kelly Whittingham. I cherish your willingness to help educators build relationships with students and improve their understanding of best practices. I applaud you. Lastly, I thank my Creator for placing such beautiful people in my life and instilling me with faith and confidence to complete this project.

Solution Tree Press would like to thank the following reviewers:

Kristen Gibson
Instructional Specialist
Pasadena Independent School District
Pasadena, Texas

Kelly Hilliard
GATE Mathematics Instructor
NBCT
Darrell C. Swope Middle School
Reno, Nevada

Ian Landy
District Principal of Technology
School District 47
Powell River, British Columbia, Canada

Paula Mathews
STEM Instructional Coach
Dripping Springs ISD
Dripping Springs, Texas

Rachel Swearengin
Fifth-Grade Teacher
Manchester Park Elementary
Lenexa, Kansas

Steven Weber
Assistant Principal
Rogers Heritage High School
Rogers, Arkansas

Visit **go.SolutionTree.com/SEL** to download the free reproducibles in this book.

Table of Contents

About the Author

Patricia Erbe is an author and former educator in Pennsylvania's West Chester Area School District, where she taught for decades at the elementary and secondary levels while also serving as a team leader, curriculum developer, science advocate, early field and student teacher mentor and consultant to individuals and organizations for professional growth and practical teaching applications. In addition to these leadership experiences, she has bolstered her social-emotional focus by leading extracurricular activities and clubs for young learners and as a consistent informal mentor for colleagues.

Furthermore, Patricia has contributed to the community through her active involvement on the West Chester Area Education Foundation Board, a nonprofit dedicated to mobilizing community resources for student benefit, and the Hopewell United Methodist Church Preschool Advisory Board. As a member of the Pennsylvania State Education Association and the Association of American Educators professional organizations, she finds staying connected to educational institutions and contemporary journals and studies critical in remaining current with educational trends and best practices.

During her career, Patricia was awarded Best Teacher of the Year and has continued to work toward elevating student potential through relationship building and keeping up with current research and educational offerings. In addition to benefiting from numerous professional development opportunities, she has assisted other educational leaders in presenting professional development seminars.

Patricia earned a bachelor's degree in elementary education from Millersville University and a master's degree (emphasizing educational development and strategies) from Wilkes University. In addition, she acquired a secondary teaching certification and has completed extensive coursework in social-emotional learning.

Introduction

I believe the end goal of education is academic, social, and emotional success for each student. Although it is not a game, we teachers can correlate teaching to a dance of sorts, with steps that include our formal education, professional development, teaching experience, content expertise, and life events. Sometimes, the tune changes, and then we adjust how we teach. Much like dance music, the practice of teaching has its high and low notes. Its melody, the most essential component, is the teacher-student relationship. Yet, it is often taken for granted.

Even though teaching is rewarding, we all know it can also be complex and daunting. Amid our daily activities and challenges, there is a tendency to neglect the monumentally important human element—the teacher-student relationship. If cultivated and nurtured, this bond brings forth life in the form of motivation and engagement, naturally leading to student self-efficacy, trust, well-being, and achievement. The onus is on us—each teacher—from kindergarten on. Students each have an extensive family of educators who share their individual lives and lessons. This "teacher force field" is enormous, and it is why an intentional effort to build solid, safe, and positive teacher-studentrelationships is necessary. It is also essential to know ourselves in terms of our brand—what makes us unique—to be effective. Just like CPR can save a life, *c*ultivating *p*ositive *r*elationships can mean the difference between a student having an exceptional education or not, the effects of which continue well past the school years.

In tandem with subject matter, students desperately need emotional ties to their teachers and a sense of belonging. The feeling of acceptance is what drives learning. Students who experience an attachment to their teachers and feel valued are more apt to view school as a positive and safe place and engage in learning (Furrer & Skinner, 2003). In addition to behavioral and emotional issues, equity gaps can be lessened with intentional efforts in relationship building (Bergin & Bergin, 2009).

It has been proposed that a genuine sense of belonging is almost as crucial to survival as one of our necessities for survival: food (Baumeister & Leary, 1995). It is not so farfetched. Water, shelter, fire, and food allow humans to live. Belonging is a separate piece, but also critical. In the film *Cast Away* (Zemeckis, 2000), Chuck Noland, played by Tom Hanks, lives on a desert island with basic survival elements but no human contact. He rescues a washed-up soccer ball, paints a face on it, and names it Wilson. Noland's essential needs relate to his physical survival but also his mental well-being. Sometimes, our students feel as if they are alone on an island too. Young learners are in a world of rapid change where they must navigate technological advancements and deteriorating societal and domestic structures, which can lead to trauma, anxiety, and depression, (Allen, Kern, Rozek, McInerney, & Slavich, 2021). A remedy does exist. Through neurological studies, we know that relationships formed between individuals and among groups help to activate oxytocin in the brain (Bosch & Young, 2017). It is a powerful hormone that helps regulate emotions and social competencies (Yoon & Kim, 2022). Knowing the importance of human connections, educators have a considerable duty to each student to be purposeful in crafting these relationships for both immediate and lifelong benefits.

This book uses decades of peer-reviewed research and professional educator experience to build the raft and rescue your students from their lonely island. At the end of our time together, you will have learned a thorough and effective strategy for establishing the right relationship with your students to ensure their emotional, social, and educational success.

Key Factors to Consider as We Begin to Establish Relationships With Students

Establishing relationships with students is more than just content knowledge. Other considerations include the level you teach, your particular students, the school community, administration, district initiatives, standards and practices, and professional development. When setting up a concrete plan to build bonds with young people, piecemeal does not work, nor does one-size-fits-all.

For example, practices for forging relationships may change from primary grades through high school due to factors such as peer influence, growth in maturity, and increased independence. Even though relationships are crucial for all levels, the processes can be more complicated with secondary students. Each teacher has less opportunity to meet each student's emotional needs due to typically larger class sizes and students seeing multiple teachers in a day (Roorda et al., 2017). Middle and high school teachers may see a student for only forty to sixty minutes per day; itinerant and specialized teachers have even less time.

Yet, it is still possible to forge good relations. It may mean different approaches. The key point is that secondary teachers cannot assume their students do not need cultivated relationships as they grow more independent. On the contrary, older students need harmonious teacher-student relationships as much as elementary students. This may necessitate using creative approaches outside the formal class period, such as interacting on district social media (sanctioned by the school), attending school events, sponsoring school clubs, and more.

Whatever a student's age or ability, it is common sense that teacher training should consist of formal education and regular professional development. Even though knowledge is indisputably essential, our experiences, who we are as people, our skills at forging relationships, and our ability to reflect and change contribute significantly to our value as educators. In other words, teaching is as much an art as a science.

Professional and Personal Experiences

Public and private school teachers across the United States have approximately fourteen years of teaching experience (Walker, 2018). In addition, between 2011 and 2021, there is no significant difference in the range of teaching experience in the public school sector, holding steady between ten and twenty years, according to the National Center for Education Statistics (2023). This would indicate we have teachers who know how to teach, manage a classroom, deal with various learning anomalies, grow professionally, and mentor others, right? One would think so, but the truth is that teaching experience alone does not make teachers exemplary.

Beyond professional preparation, we bring the breadth of our life experiences from childhood through adulthood into the classroom, and they can hinder or help our relationships with students. There are days when we come to school with our lives in upheaval. However, projecting this onto our students is costly and can get in the way of positive relationships. Consider this: we might even use stressful circumstances to improve how students perceive us and, by doing so, create a more favorable impression, or brand, for ourselves. Letting students know when we are going through a tough time can dissolve any misperceptions they may have about us. This can result in stronger bonds with our students and perhaps even an emotional lift for ourselves. Being honest with students can help—with discretion, of course.

Purposeful Self-Reflection

From research, experience, and pure gut instinct, I am confident that the relationship cultivated with each student is the *primary* factor contributing to their positive school experience and the best possible outcome. Having that in mind, let's be honest. Do you know your students? I mean, truly know them. Do you use that knowledge in tandem with instructing them? Are you happy with your teaching career? Are there areas where you feel the need for improvement? Do you predict that this book will be more of the same because you have been professionally *over*developed? Are you reading this book on your own accord or because your employer requires you to do so? Are you just curious? Have you thought about quitting the profession because your impact on students seems limited?

Knowledge and experience are undeniably essential. However, we must know our strengths and weaknesses, understand the nuances of relationships, and have a concrete plan to serve our students better. In short, we must brand, bond, and build for successful teacher-student relationships. I hope this book will help you in that ongoing quest.

The Teacher-Student Relationship Model

When I was a preservice teacher and taking academic courses for certification, learning about educational pioneers seemed irrelevant. Sure, we read books about educational philosophers and viewed videos of theories in action. Still, it was not easy to appreciate these concepts—that is, until I gathered field experience in an actual teaching situation. Only then did I experience firsthand the power of teacher-student relationships.

I was thrilled but a bit surprised to experience how strongly connections with students helped create ideal scenarios for them to be their best selves. Finally, the educational gurus made sense. Once I began planning lessons and teaching, I could appreciate educational experts such as Jean Piaget (Piaget & Inhelder, 1969), Jerome Bruner (1983), Lev S. Vygotsky (1978), and Howard Gardner (2011) and apply their theories to the real world of teaching and learning.

I believe there is still an insufficient emphasis on teacher-student relationships in theory and practice. First, in our increasingly data-driven profession, it is not easy to precisely define our relationships with our students and quantify how these connections influence their success. Each student is unique, each situation is unique, and each teacher-student relationship is unique. Of course, there is empirical evidence through our personal observations, feedback, reflection, and collaboration with peers, administrators, and parents to endorse and promote ideal teacher-student relationships.

To be most effective, these often-ignored skills still require an organized and practical methodology to achieve. So far, this has not existed, which is why I wrote this book. I like to think of it this way: we cannot drive on the road as we are paving it, nor can we drive on the road without direction. We need a map. Only by reflecting can we learn from our mistakes and become wiser. With that in mind, this book contains spaces for you to do just that. Therefore, please consider this book not something to *read*, but something to *do*. Have your pen ready.

Figure I.1 (page 6) provides a road map for establishing the best possible teacher-student relationships using four critical ingredients. The first three are *branding*, *bonding*, and *building*.

Your *brand* is a fusion of your personality and your passions. It is your uniqueness—what makes you different from other educators—and it is a catalyst for connecting with your students. Creating your brand means taking a self-inventory of your attributes and capitalizing on those most conducive to creating solid relationships. As you reveal your brand to your students over time, *bonding* will follow. Creating ties is influenced by your classroom environment, how you communicate, and your nurturing of inclusiveness. You will continue to strengthen your connections with your students as you *build* on your foundations of branding and bonding. A prescribed planned strategy allows the freedom to know individual students' social, emotional, and academic needs. The fourth ingredient is *reflecting*, which is vital for synthesizing and strengthening relationship branding, bonding, and building over time. All these critical ingredients are explained in more detail throughout this book.

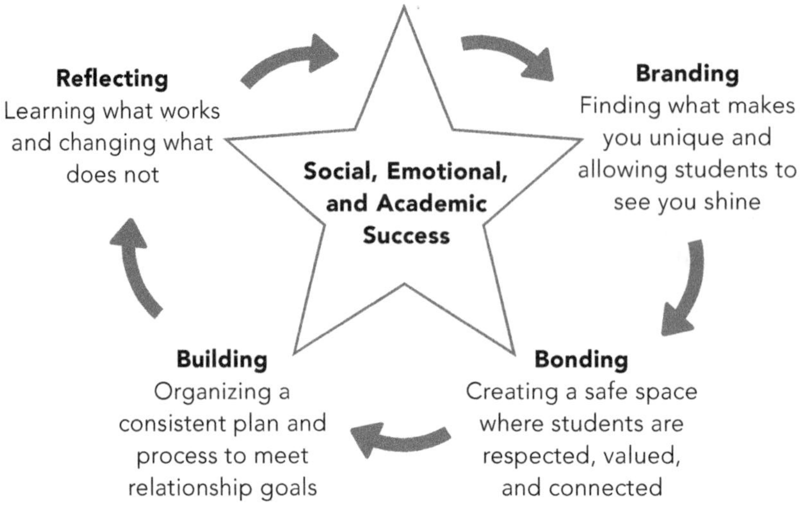

Figure I.1: Teacher-student relationship (TSR) model.

In This Book

This book is divided into three parts and each one represents a critical ingredient of the TSR model. Along with exercises to implement in your classroom, each chapter will include reflection boxes in which you can engage further with the content.

- **Part I: Brand.** Who are you as an individual and as an educator? How does this factor into forming connections?
    - **Chapter 1: Make the Right First Impression.** Your students form perceptions of you starting in the first few seconds of the first day of school. Factors such as your gestures, facial expressions, and wardrobe can impact those first impressions.
    - **Chapter 2: Create Your Brand.** Who are you as an authentic individual? What passions might you share with your students? Your brand combines who you are as a person with what you allow your students to see. How you craft this balance can make a difference in the way students perceive you.

- **Part II: Bond.** What indispensable factors should you be aware of that help you create more significant ties with your students?
    - **Chapter 3: Identify Your Community of Learners.** Your students need a learning environment where they feel welcome and accepted. Intentionally building your classroom community toward these goals will create an atmosphere that promotes respect, values individuality, and fosters connections.
    - **Chapter 4: Build Your Communication.** As you communicate with students and the school community, how you interact with others is another variable in developing relationships.
    - **Chapter 5: Support Your Students' Special Needs.** Insights from experienced special educators can help you develop relationships with students who may be academically, behaviorally, or socially challenged.
    - **Chapter 6: Cultivate Diverse Connections.** As you honor diversity and promote equity, racism and microaggressions may still surface. Self-reflection and continuing learning can help you feel more comfortable with conversations and situations as they arise.
    - **Chapter 7: Create an Inclusive Environment by Responding to Student Voices.** Although you feel comfortable with inclusivity, it is always valuable to explore new ideas for creating an accepting and equitable classroom community.
- **Part III: Build.** What scaffolding can you use to construct palpable relationships?
    - **Chapter 8: Design Your TSR Model.** You are in charge. As you design your teacher-student relationship strategies, a step-by-step guide can facilitate creating meaningful connections with students.
- **Epilogue: Reflect for Self-Efficacy and Change.** The practice of reflecting is one of your most powerful professional habits. Revisiting your curriculum, instructional practices, and attitudes

on a regular basis can enhance your teaching and, most important, enrich your bonds with your students.

As you can see, this book will examine many angles that play into developing favorable relationships with students. To begin, consider where you stand with student relationships in your classroom. Let your reflections become your discoveries, and your findings be your map to creating more meaningful teacher experiences. Enjoy the journey!

What were some successes you have experienced with developing and maintaining teacher-student relationships? What were some challenges?

PART I

BRAND

The following pages reveal how your uniqueness is a catalyst for connecting with your students. Learn how body language, personality, mannerisms, and methodology create your *brand* and how they set you apart from your colleagues.

1

Make the Right First Impression

I've learned that people will forget what you said, people will forget what you did, but people will never forget how you made them feel.
—Maya Angelou

It is astounding how quickly students form opinions of their teachers. As a middle school teacher, I recall many first days of school when students would enter my classroom talking with one another about how they did not like some of their assigned teachers. How could this be? They had been together only fifty minutes. There is an explanation for why students create snap judgments; *physiognomy* is the study of psychological expressions involving the face and body. Princeton University researchers concluded that we judge facial expressions within a hundred milliseconds, and subsequent assumptions are strengthened or changed as more information about a person is introduced (Willis & Todorov, 2006). Even experts in body language believe it takes only seconds for our spoken words and demeanor to form the basis of how students perceive us (Pease & Pease, 2006). What we say, how we move, and sometimes what we wear contribute to students' first impressions. A negative initial encounter is not easily overturned. It takes multiple positive interactions to counterbalance them (Demaris & White, 2004). This is not to scare you but to reinforce that your first encounter with students holds enormous importance.

Aside from the fact first impressions form in the blink of an eye, *how* do they occur? Behavioral and communications expert Mark Bowden (2013) believes your body language places you in one of three categories when someone meets you: friend, enemy, or neither (indifferent). As humans, our innate goal is to make it into the friend group. However, this does not mean you must be friends with your students. You are still the one in charge, and you have boundaries. Bowden's (2013) reference to friends simply means you want to be seen positively instead of as mean-spirited, apathetic, or threatening. How to accomplish this? It includes practicing positive body language and voice inflections to impact the first impression you create for your students. Think of all the time you spend developing and revamping lessons, applying best practices, and completing professional development. Given all this, it makes sense to practice putting your best self forward in the classroom. It is the beginning of a relationship. Just as you use fewer muscles to smile than to frown, it takes less effort to create a great first impression than to try and overturn a negative one later.

That said, when it comes to being perceived positively, we must be positive and forgiving with ourselves. Suppose the first day goes poorly, and you find yourself stammering with particulars and procedures. All is not lost. If students see you as nervous or unprepared, reflect on that and figure out how to improve the next day. The key is to accept that you are not perfect. The difference between sinking and sailing is your willingness to admit your mistakes and make a positive change the next time. If you drop the first impression anchor from the boat into the muck, it does not mean you cannot pull the anchor back up and continue sailing.

Picture this: you begin to introduce yourself to your class. How are you standing? Are you moving around? Where have you positioned yourself in relationship to the students? Are your hands empty or holding papers or cards to remind you of what to say? Are your arms folded? What are you wearing? Are your clothes colorful or neutral? What kind of expressions do you think you are displaying? How are you greeting the students as they come into class, or are you not greeting them? These questions may seem minor, but they determine how you will be perceived.

In *The Definitive Book of Body Language*, Allan Pease and Barbara Pease (2006) explain how you influence others through more than your words. Through their research, you can learn more about the importance of projecting the best of yourself to your students. As you will see, everything from your head to your feet can convey messages. In this chapter, you will learn how your hands, arms, eyes, smile, stance, voice, and even your clothing factor into your students' first impression of you and how cultural differences can influence those interpretations. At the end of the chapter (page 21), you'll find a reproducible guide to basic body language and accompanying meanings.

Your Hands and Arms

To express sincerity, pay attention to your hands and arms. Open and outward hands with palms exposed imply truthfulness and say, "Welcome to my classroom!" Conversely, showing the back of your hands and concealing your palms can give an authoritarian appearance. You want students to know who is in charge, but you do not want your students to think of you as a dictator and become afraid. Finally, even though you use your index finger to point as a communication tool at times, using it along with a harsh voice, mean-spirited words, or negative facial expressions can convey aggression (Taylor, 2023). A better practice is only using your finger as a pointer, such as giving instructions or directions.

Sometimes, teachers greet students with a handshake, elbow bump, or fist bump. However, there are positive and negative ways to do this. For example, a handshake can express different signals. A palm facing upward says, "I have the power." Your palm facing downward means, "I am giving away the power." Finally, a straight palm, neither up nor down, shows equality. In terms of the grip strength, it should be equal on both sides. If you hold on more tightly than your student, simply lighten your hold. Small handshake nuances can make the difference between your students viewing you as friendly or fearsome.

Aside from the handshake, your hands speak loudly for you in other ways. Clenched together, your hands demonstrate frustration. Rubbing your hands together is an optimistic gesture, meaning you see positive outcomes in the future. Placing your fingertips together like a steeple shows confidence.

Since we are discussing hands, I would be remiss not to mention touching. Some schools or districts prohibit any touching of students, while others may allow small interactions such as fist bumps. Make sure you are aware of your specific rules on appropriate touch. I know it can be difficult because students sometimes run and hug you, especially if you are a beloved teacher. Make sure you know how to handle that in advance through the guidance of your school policies. Folding your arms across your chest as if you are protecting your vital organs connotes negativity or defensiveness to your students. You are showing insecurity if you grip your arms with your hands folded across your body like a hug. The same goes for the one-arm grab or partial arm cross, when you have one arm straight at your side and grab it with your other arm across your body. Self-doubt and insecurity are not things you want to show your students, especially when creating a first impression. Think of the consequences for you.

So, where do you place your hands and arms to show your openness and authority? Experts say to extend your arms with your palms facing outward toward your listeners. In this way, you reveal confidence and positive power.

Remember, body language elements work together. You cannot display proper hand or arm placement with a scowl on your face and a negative tone in your voice and still expect to come across in a positive light. Subtle movements make all the difference in how students perceive you.

Your Eyes and Brows

In one-fifth of a second, you can send a signal that will read as "friendly." Simply raise your eyebrows upwards, wrinkling your forehead into lines as quickly as possible, and then relax your forehead. Try it. This gesture takes very little energy yet can pack a punch when you try to convince others that you are someone to be trusted. To show others that you are friendly and nonthreatening, use what is known as a *flash brow*, a quick up and down signal by the forehead that engages those making eye contact (Van Edwards, n.d.). Even in a study with infants, researchers concluded that babies show interest by locking their eyes when seeing a flash brow (Senju & Csibra, 2008). No matter what your brows may be doing, they work naturally in tandem with your eyes. How about the famous "teacher stare"? You know the one—the lowered eyes coupled with furrowed brows. This conveys disappointment. I prefer eyes wide open and a friendly gaze.

Speaking of the eyes, these silent communicators cannot be underrated. There is a designated name for the study of how the eyes move and communicate: oculesics (Andersen, 2016). In education, teachers tend to talk a lot about the eyes in terms of student eye contact. In this regard, teachers strive to ensure each student looks at them as they teach because it indicates students are engaged and learning. However, there is more potential to the eyes than you may realize. Eye contact is only one of three eye expression categories. Eye movement is the second, including the rolling of eyes, which you are familiar with. Another example is what if you want to tell your instructional aide in your classroom to keep an eye on a student? Instead of speaking, you may gain eye contact and move your eyes toward the student's direction. Eye movement cues are indispensable to teachers in the classroom, especially when trying to be discreet (Bowman & Compton, 2022). A third eye expression is pupil dilation. Your pupils expand when light is dim, allowing as much light as possible to enter the eye. Conversely, when there is too much light, pupils contract. Some other factors, such as health issues or drugs, can change the size of pupils and cause them to dilate or contract involuntarily in response to anxiety (Folk, 2021). You could consult a medical professional, such as the school nurse, if you have concerns about a student exhibiting a dilated pupil pattern.

Your Smile

Are you authentic? Your smile will show it. The more that smiling occurs, the more positive the reception. That said, your smile must be genuine. Imagine you are meeting a student for the first time. As they approach, you notice an angry face and a messy look. Without thinking, you fold your arms and step back with one foot. Since it is the first day of school, you force a smile and try to make it sincere. Your body language does not match your smile, so presenting yourself this way is confusing.

A natural smile is when the corners of the mouth curl upwards and the sides of the eyes crinkle. A fake smile is when the mouth is stretched across and not upward. Remember, your smile should match the other attributes you display to others, such as how you present your hands, palms, stance, and tone of voice. Otherwise, you will not appear to be sincere. And young people can spot a phony a mile away.

Your Stance

In meeting your students for the first time, where do you think you should stand in proximity to them? Standing directly in front of someone can indicate aggression. Thus, try to position yourself in front of your students at an angle, creating openness and revealing a more confident stance. Students will feel more comfortable because you are signaling them to ask questions and participate. You don't want to appear rigid or too loose. Remember to watch the positioning of your feet. Always hold your head high and straighten your posture, but not too stiffly. Standing straight without rigidity, shoulders square, and head up shows confidence, whereas slumping over with head down expresses the opposite.

Your Clothing

Everyone has their own style of clothing. Some teachers like to keep up with clothing trends, while others gravitate toward more traditional attire. After all, we are all individuals. Yet, research on apparel shows that a person's clothing speaks loudly and clearly to the perceiver, even without verbal communication (Howlett et al., 2013; Wei et al., 2017). However, specific school practices may influence how best to convey positivity. For example, on the first day of school, all teachers at my school wear the school polo shirt to signify unity. Although casual dress can indicate a lack of leadership or authority, its effect may not be the same for a collective dress-down day and, of course, may also differ based on the subject taught (such as physical education or art).

Adding to the complexity of clothes and first impressions is the concept of color perception among cultures. For example, orange is the national color of the Netherlands and its royal family, whereas it is part of the grieving process in Egypt (Grzybowski & Kupidura-Majewski, 2019). These variances should be considered, especially when the makeup of a class is diverse. It is unclear whether wearing specific colors affects cultural perceptions and conclusions about someone's personality. However, the takeaway is there are so many variables regarding color's effect on human judgment that it may not make a difference unless a particular color is worn consistently.

That said, there is no "best look" for educators. What you wear speaks to your personality and is part of the brand you build. Whereas more formal attire garners more credibility, the opposite occurs the more casual and informally dressed one may be (Dunbar & Segrin, 2012). Strike a balance. Also, you may want to avoid clothes that are too tight or revealing or a color that does not match your personality. Others may judge you based on your clothes and colors, but you are not the sum of what your clothes and the colors speak of you. Many other factors contribute to how your students perceive you.

Your Voice

The tone of your voice and your words work with nonverbal language to convey your honesty, authenticity, and integrity. To deliver a clear and honest message, be straightforward and precise with your words to avoid hurting another's feelings. Authenticity is essential because it contributes to your reliability. Mirror your unique principles and beliefs. Say what you feel and do what you say. This is a process over a lifetime—learning and adjusting for the next encounter with people and relationships (Henry, 2016). By being true to yourself, you will gain more integrity and stronger bonds with all. So how do you use your voice in the best way possible? You must express positivity to avoid the "seven deadly sins" that destroy credibility: gossip, judging, negativity, complaining, excuses, lying, and dogmatism (Treasure, 2013). Avoiding these shows that you care for your students. In turn, students will know they are valued and loved, leading to their trust and respect.

Extremes in vocal tone can cause students, or even colleagues, to shy away from what you are saying, affecting your relationship with them. Best practices are to speak from your chest rather than the nasal passages or throat. Provide a warm, silky tone to your voice, and for goodness' sake, stay away from being monotone. Remember *Ferris Bueller's Day Off* (Hughes, 1986)? "Bueller, Bueller, Bueller. Anyone, anyone, anyone?" The teacher in that movie provided strong examples of what not to do. Avoid droning or sing-song levels in your voice, and keep inflections varied at the end of each sentence instead of raising your voice upward repetitively as if you are asking a question. Keep your voice measured, emphasizing necessary points appropriately. Remember that it is best to pause without "ums" and "ahs." Your voice should undulate gently with variation and richness.

Cultural Considerations

Because classrooms include students of diverse cultural backgrounds, it is vital to be aware of cultural nuances in body language. We do not want to offend our students, nor do we want to create misunderstandings. For example, in many Western cultures, making direct eye contact signifies respect or engagement. However, in some countries like Japan or China, looking directly into another's eyes can be unnerving and disrespectful. It is considered more polite to lower the eyes (Scroope & Evason, 2017; Scroope, 2021). Hand gestures may also have a variety of connotations. For instance, teachers may use the thumbs-up sign to mean "OK" or "good job." However, in France, the same gesture can indicate the number one (Danon, 2019). And in some primarily Islamic countries such as Iraq, Afghanistan, and Iran, it can have a very offensive meaning (Anderson et al., 2019). There are countless other ways that your body language may not always convey what you assume it does. It is especially important to think twice about judging your students' expressions and demeanor based on your cultural context. Overall, creating a culturally responsive classroom environment is the goal, and honoring differences in ways of interacting contributes to that end. If you are curious about other body language interpretations throughout the world, head to websites such as www.culturalatlas.com where you will find cultural differences, gestures, and their meanings.

Active Self-Awareness

Body language awareness is vital but does not stand alone because you convey multiple expressions, seemingly all at once. For instance, a smile happens along with the placement of your hands or arms, voice, and stance. If you smile with the mouth corners upward but with furrowed brows and a scowl, students may judge you as insincere.

Not only do body language movements work together to reveal information but also students' experiences and preconceived notions of you also serve as nonverbal indicators, providing insights about you. You may remind a student of someone else in a particular way. Have you ever heard that a student is happy to be in your class because their brother, sister, neighbor, or friend previously enjoyed it? Sometimes, your students have ideas about you before setting foot in your room.

The crux lies in authenticity, whether or not students know who you are before their first encounter with you. Awareness of all nonverbal information about you is essential in providing students with the most precise picture.

How can you make sure you display a genuine approach? One suggestion is to practice by recording your first day welcome speech in front of a mirror. What will you say? How will you show the students who you are and how you feel about them? What are the most critical feelings you want to evoke? How will you project inclusiveness? Try playing it back and scrutinizing your movements and words. Take notes. Where could you have improved? Maybe sharing the video with a family member, friend, or colleague to get input would produce practical advice.

Creating a strengths and weaknesses list can be helpful too. How often do you make others feel appreciated, smile, and listen to what they have to say? Do you inspire others through your words and interaction? Be aware of your movements, especially during those first few moments in meeting your students. Most likely, you prepared for your first teaching interview. Perhaps you practiced interviewing with a friend, researched the school district or institution, or tweaked your résumé. On the day of the meeting, maybe you reviewed, generated a few practice questions, dressed presentably, and talked yourself into feeling confident as you drove to the interview location. Because the job was important to you, you were inspired to prepare in many ways. Ask yourself: How was the interview process different or more important than meeting your students for the first time?

Conclusion

With all these suggestions, you may be feeling overwhelmed, and you are not alone. I felt that way too. I suggest selecting a few body movements, vocal techniques, or specific words you would like to focus on and try them out. Word to the wise—make sure you are yourself. Learning more about all the ways you communicate nonverbally cannot be minimized.

Indeed, the science behind how we communicate and its application can be mind-boggling; however, it is possible. Presenting the best of yourself through your actions (and words) can create a positive relationship with each student—at first and then over time. It takes patience and systematic planning. After the first impression stage is when students learn about you as a teacher and person. This is where you begin to reveal the true you—your brand.

Select a few body movements of interest in the following "Body Language Chart" reproducible and reflect on your relationship with them. How can you use them effectively in the classroom?

Body Language Chart

Action	Implication	
	Hands	
Assertive handshake	Upper hand positioning shows confidence	
Passive handshake	Shaking hands with palms upward relinquishes control	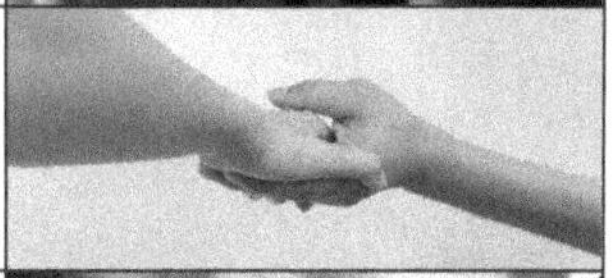
Mutual handshake	Both hands in equal position generates respect	
Tight fist hand	Suppressing negative energy	
Pressing hands	Back and forth motion of hands demonstrates a hopeful mindset	
Finger pyramid	Exhibits positivity and confidence, but negative if coupled with other negative signs	
Upward palm	Signifies harmless and approachable	
Downward palm	Domineering with the possibility of hostility	
Index finger	When using to point, can show negativity unless presenting information for clarification	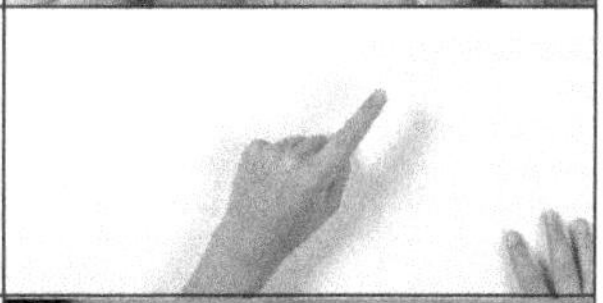
Fingers tucked with thumb on top	Illustrates control, nonaggressive	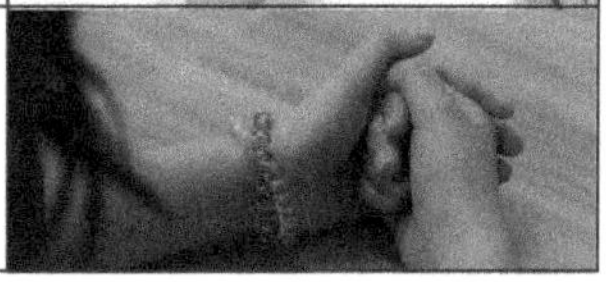

page 1 of 4

Action	Implication	
	Arms	
Chest crossed	Feeling negative vibes, insecurity, need for protection	
Semi chest-crossed	Arm L-shaped across body holding opposite arm indicates lack of confidence	
Extended palms outward	Both arms extended, palms facing out indicate honesty and openness	
Posterior	Both arms behind back, hands clasped shows one is in command	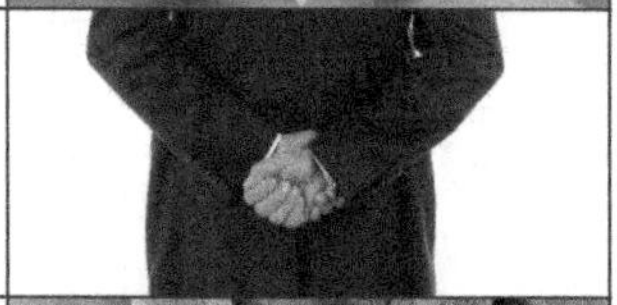
One-armed posterior	Arms behind the back with hands clasped and holding wrist of the other arm depicts frustration	
	Smile	
Common	Corners of mouth upward, eyes wrinkled at corners indicate sincerity	
Restraint	Mouth stretched corner to corner, no teeth shown indicates insincerity, hidden agenda	
Crooked	Lips stretched at angle, corners pushed down or up (smirk) indicate sarcasm	

Action	Implication	
	Eyes and Brows	
Lowered	Represents dishonesty or displeasure, and sometimes authority	
Raised	Wide eyes indicate a look of surprise	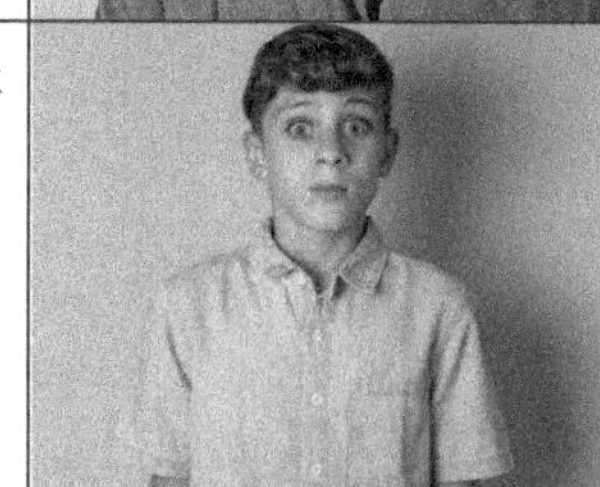
Mid-raised	Brows together and upward present astonishment or amazement	
Mid-lowered	Brows pulled together and downward shows focus or irritation	
Mid-together	Illustrates misconception or bewilderment	
Quick lift	An instantaneous shift of eyebrows up then down conveys interest and positivity	

Action	Implication	
	Stance	
Forward	Standing at an angle, feet pointed toward listener shows engagement	
Distant	Standing or positioning a foot away from listener indicates the desire to leave	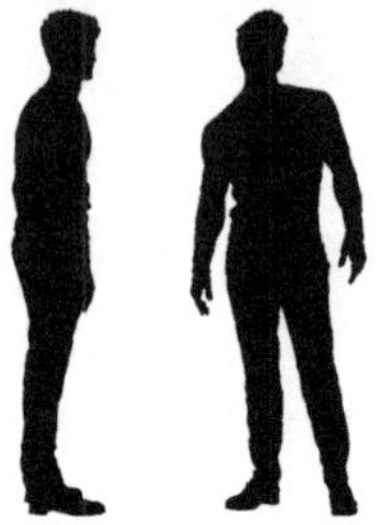
Inclusive	People standing while allowing space for another to join	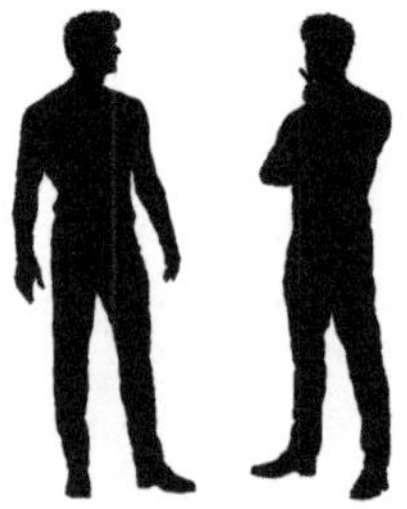
Noninclusive	Triad or more of people standing who do not allow any room for another to join	

Source: Adapted from Cuncic, A. (2023, March 28). How to read facial expressions. Accessed at https://verywellmind.com/understanding-emotions-through-facial-expressions-3024851#How%20to%20Identify%20Facial%20Expressions%20by%20Facial%20 Feature on March 27, 2024; Navarro, J. (2018). The dictionary of body language: A field guide to human behavior. New York: HarperCollins; Pease, A., & Pease, B. (2006). The definitive book of body language. New York: Bantam Books.

2

Create Your Brand

Our job is to connect to people, to interact with them in a way that leaves them better than we found them, more able to get where they'd like to go.
—Seth Godin

At first, it may seem a bit odd for a teacher to have a brand. However, there is a strong correlation between marketing products and teaching students. Both functions require planning, resourcefulness, and innovation to achieve positive results. Corporations rely on strong branding to increase recognition, create favorable impressions, and improve outcomes. Think, for example, of Apple's well-known apple logo or Nike's swoosh and "Just Do It" slogan. All are part of ongoing strategies to craft a positive brand identity. Teaching is not that much different.

In general, a personal brand is being uniquely you and the best person you can be. Your "best" brand will become the glue that binds you to your students. In fact, a dedicated business publication, *Forbes*, featured an article titled "Why Teachers Need a Personal Brand and How to Create One" (Shulman, 2019). It quoted author Marietta Gentles Crawford, who broadly defines a *personal brand* as the "sum of your strengths and characteristics that are unique to you" (Shulman, 2019). Crawford advised being aware of your "reputation management. . . consistently showing unique attributes in everything you do, in-person and online" (Shulman, 2019).

In the same way a brand can help a company succeed, your teaching brand can directly affect your ability to connect with your students and encourage their achievements. What you display and what you say form the image your students have of you. Therefore, getting to know more about yourself, what you offer, and how you project yourself to others is vital in growing a positive brand. Just as solid brands bring value to companies, the brand you create affects your value as an educator. Each of your characteristics matters. For instance, a teacher who is inflexible or passive in their approach to forging positive relationships may not choose to grow or may need more tools or insight to change. Their unbendable nature to try and change can be overshadowed by any other positive attributes about them.

With a winning reputation based on all your unique qualities, you are more likely to establish a strong relationship with your students. Because the goal is for our students to succeed, offering the best of yourself in your brand portfolio is the best way to make this happen.

Conduct Self-Research on Your Brand

Presumably, you were drawn to education for a reason and decided to take the formal leap to become a teacher. I asked several colleagues why they became teachers. One said that as a child, she often played pretend school. She found that she loved being in charge and helping others her age or younger to learn. Another said that while was growing up, he always seemed to find himself in leadership positions, teaching sports to others in his circle of friends. In my earlier years, I was my neighborhood's favorite babysitter. We all displayed a love for children and teaching that was reinforced by family members and friends who witnessed teacher-type characteristics within us. The words *kindness*, *resourcefulness*, *control*, and *knowledge* surfaced as we talked about our paths to teaching. These adjectives describe many in the profession. The following writing prompt and workspace will help you identify which of your personality traits you most want to exhibit to your students.

Creating your brand also means understanding your passions. This could mean leadership responsibilities in your school, community involvement, travel experiences, heritage, hobbies, talents, and even your family. If you are stuck, reach out to friends and family who know you best. Sometimes, others see us better than we see ourselves.

What are the personality traits you possess that you wish to share with your students? Create a list.

Your brand is everything that makes you exclusively you. Your characteristics, talents, connections, hobbies, and interests are valuable gifts you can share with young learners to enrich your interactions. Use the following writing prompt and workspace to brainstorm the kind of traits that others tend to notice about you.

What things are you known for other than the grade level or subjects you teach? You may find it beneficial to ask for input from others who know you best.

Infuse Elements of Yourself Into Your Teaching

A former colleague who taught elementary school was passionate about thematic teaching, or a specific topic of focus woven across all content areas within a particular unit. This teacher taught artfully and thoughtfully with kindness and compassion every day. Students cared for numerous animals in her classroom, Shakespeare was a regular, and students were actively engaged every moment. She was overtly passionate about ensuring her students learned in a worldly fashion. Even though her dynamic approach was unconventional, I am confident her students learned a great deal in their time with her. Over the years, I have spoken with some of her former students, and all have beautiful memories of being in her classroom. Her particular and unique flair for teaching shone brightly, and her students were forever impacted positively.

While teaching middle school, I had the pleasure of working with an outstanding teacher whose brand influenced his out-of-the-box methodology. For instance, he brought history alive by dressing up as characters from the American Revolution. Of course, not every teacher can be an actor, but remember, this was *his* passion. There was always a lot of excitement when he went into character, and his efforts inspired authentic learning. Students may forget his name in time, but they will never forget the teacher who portrayed historical figures. That is what branding does. Your unique passion imparts knowledge into students' brains and strengthens relationships with them, facilitating their learning.

Sometimes, the value added to our teaching is subtle. Another middle school colleague had an affinity for sports, and her love for baseball and football was a force in her teaching. She proudly displayed her extensive baseball bobblehead collection on her classroom shelves each year after taking them carefully from their individual boxes. These seemingly inconspicuous and whimsical models of actual players made immediate connections with her sports-minded students. She wove sports into her teaching through in-class activities, examples, and games. After each weekend, she connected with students by discussing their favorite teams' scores and key plays. She let her students know that her role in the classroom was as their coach, and they were the players working as a team. She emphasized that sports are not just games, but relationships with others and working together for common goals. She drove home the simile with: Working hard in school is like practicing a sport. One may not win the game each time because everyone makes mistakes, but when you make mistakes, work harder and learn from them. Yet, her passion for sports was only part of her value-added repertoire and brand. She loved music, incorporated it into her English lessons, and encouraged her students to do the same in their projects. I am sure she will be known for more passions, but these two stood out.

A strategy to integrate your interests into your teaching is to start by selecting just one thing you especially enjoy. Look at the personality traits you have listed in the previous prompts so far in this chapter. The points you have written down are what you could use to inject your lessons and daily interactions. Suppose you have a deep affection for animals. I have seen colleagues use their cat or dog as a class mascot by using their name or picture in lessons and almost personifying their pet to make connections. Just like the teacher who loved to dress up in period garb for each unit in his history class to engage students and bond with them or the teacher who used sports teams as one of her platforms, you can create a distinctive brand too.

If the personal interest idea seems foreign and you struggle to connect with your students by using your uniqueness as a guide, take heart. Instead, discover the interests of your *students* and assist them in creating ties with one another, which can be used in tandem with the curriculum you teach. This can be done simply by having the students nominate some of their favorite passions (perhaps ten), and you write them as the headers on a chart. For example, the likelihood of nominations such as *sports* or *video games* is a fair assumption. Students could then sign their name under all topics that interest them. Ideally, it would be best to project this from a computer but using a manual method of chart paper with headings placed around the room, allowing students to sign their name, will work. Either way, this activity creates a display of shared interests to weave into your lessons. At the core of this activity, you will learn more about your students, be able to connect with them more personally, and communicate with them differently while strengthening your relationship with them.

Keep a Holistic View of Your Identity

One word of caution: on the flip side, negative attributes can also become part of your brand if you are not careful. Don't be known as the teacher who is impatient and constantly sending misbehaving students to the hall or office, who does not listen to students, or who is unapproachable. Of course, you can still have a day when you lose your patience or wish you could have acted differently. We all make mistakes at times. And while sharing personal side stories can create powerful connections, make sure they are appropriate. It is acceptable to share the adventures of your pet dog or cat, but not OK if you share the details of your wild weekend. Be careful what you post on social media too. Your students may be watching. Use common sense, and if you are unsure if you should share something, run it by your administrator or team leader. The main idea here is that you share and show positive qualities regularly. That is what makes an exceptional brand and an outstanding teacher.

Aside from what makes us unique, there are attributes we can share mutually. Many schools teach the six pillars of character: trustworthiness, respect, responsibility, fairness, caring, and citizenship. These summations of "basic values" were established in 1992 (at the Josephson Institute in Aspen, Colorado) by educators and many youth leaders nationwide who researched what makes good character and developed "best practices" to address social-emotional learning (SEL) needs for young learners. Take a peek at the guiding principles or foundation for the CHARACTER COUNTS! program (Ray Center at Drake University, 2020):

1. The next generation will be the stewards of our communities, nation, and planet in extraordinarily critical times.
2. In such times, the well-being of our society requires an involved, caring citizenry with good moral character.
3. People do not automatically develop good moral character; therefore, conscientious efforts must be made to help young people develop the values and abilities necessary for moral decision making and conduct.
4. Effective character education is based on core ethical values rooted in a democratic society, in particular, respect, responsibility, trustworthiness, justice, and fairness, caring and civic virtue, and citizenship.
5. These core ethical values transcend cultural, religious, and socioeconomic differences.
6. Character education is, first and foremost, an obligation of families and faith communities, but schools and youth-service organizations also have a responsibility to help develop the character of young people.
7. These responsibilities are best achieved when these groups work in concert.
8. The character and conduct of our youth reflect the character and conduct of society; therefore, every adult has the responsibility to teach and model the core ethical values and every social institution has the responsibility to promote the development of good character.

No matter whether you use a program at your school or not, there is merit in students, teachers, and all adults in education abiding by these eight core principles. They can be incorporated into the rules of the classroom along with discipline and consequences, as well as reinforced through daily activities and lessons. The CHARACTER COUNTS! website (https://charactercounts.org) has a plethora of lesson plans and curriculum resources to offer should you need ideas or support.

I have often heard teachers say, "Follow the golden rule," to their students, which is only useful if students understand what that means. I think they need to be taught more than to *do unto others as you would have done unto you.* Students need to see their teacher modeling values—actively and purposefully—throughout the year. In using character development as a teacher-student (not just student) framework in the classroom, you create another identity for yourself—a dynamic positive leader, who students look up to, admire, and follow. Your actions and words will build your relationships and assist students in developing better social-emotional skills, which can be very powerful.

Enhance Your Brand

So far, we have looked at the meaning and examples of branding, and you might have a sense of how to define and craft your brand. Let us ponder some questions to guide you in creating, enhancing, or even revamping your brand. Use the following workspace to jot or mind map your thoughts about these fundamental questions:

- Who are you? What are some words to describe your personality?
- What are some of your teacher-type characteristics, like how you execute the subject matter you teach, how you communicate with your students, or your discipline practices?
- What are you passionate about in your career?
- What are you enthusiastic about outside of school in your personal life?
- How do you inspire and engage your students?
- What sets you apart from others? You may have qualities in common with colleagues, but what is unique about you specifically?
- What is your "added value" or special attributes you share with students, peers, school, and community?

Reflect on what makes you unique and consider some daily goals to live up to the expectations you have set for yourself. Your students will appreciate you more, and you will feel more confident about relationship-building in your classroom. Use the following prompt and workspace to self-search your brand.

To better understand yourself and your brand, consider the guiding questions and generate a physical representation of your personality, uniqueness, and any relationship-building goals you wish to implement in the classroom. Start with a personal mind map using online map tools, a notepad, or a journal.

Conclusion

Realizing your brand requires thought and sometimes input from others to discover your maximum relationship-building potential. Looking inwardly at your gifts and strengths may add value to your connection efforts with students. Consider how friends, family, and colleagues perceive you as a person and educator. Find new insights from their input and choose traits you wish to project as your brand to help form positive relationships.

Team up with your students and create a "we" atmosphere of getting to know one another better. Students can be involved in finding each other's talents and unique qualities and then share their interests and passions with the other students and with you. Another mutual way to connect with young learners is to focus on the six pillars of character of trustworthiness, respect, responsibility, fairness, caring, and citizenship through teacher modeling and collaborative lessons.

Understanding yourself and your students better and allowing them to see you more transparently will help create a first-rate classroom experience. Chapter 3 (page 37) builds on this foundation and gives you more ideas on developing a winning classroom community learning environment—an integral part of building and sustaining solid relationships.

PART II

BOND

Over time, as you reveal your brand to your students, bonding will follow. The next chapters dive into the specifics of classroom community, communication, and inclusiveness and how their impact is critical in establishing relationships and helping you create a village of trust, openness, and acceptance.

3

Identify Your Community of Learners

When everyone in the classroom, teacher and students, recognizes that they are responsible for creating a learning community together, learning is at its most meaningful and useful.
—bell hooks

You start to create your classroom community on day one. After you greet your students at the door and they form their initial feelings about you, their second impressions happen when they enter your classroom. Immediately, they size up its look and feel. At that moment, the visual stimuli unconsciously make your students feel emotions on a spectrum from uneasy to comfortable. Therefore, it is crucial to consider the content and placement of all items in your room. What does your environment—their classroom home—look like? How does it feel?

Over the years, I visited many classrooms that felt incredibly welcoming and others, not so much. For example, on one professional development day, my colleagues and I reported to one of our district's high school classrooms. Even though it was a warm October and a month into the school year, the room felt cold and hollow. Three bulletin boards stood entirely naked, and the fourth bore only a single calendar and procedural papers. The only objects were the teacher's nameplate on the door, the United States flag at the front of the room, and pieces of blue tape on the floor for aligning desks. That was it.

However, simply adding objects to walls and surfaces is not the best solution either. On another professional development day, we met in a middle school classroom. In the assigned room, wall hangings and pictures covered every inch of the concrete block walls without any sense of arrangement. Papers were in disarray on a rectangular table near the teacher's desk, and student desks were askew. It made me uneasy, and I am in no way a perfectionist.

A balanced and inviting classroom should be organized, engaging, and dynamic. It is a good idea to personalize it, with moderation, of course. Students are observant and look for clues that indicate a safe and welcoming environment. But they also seek hints about you, and your classroom is a sneak peek into your personality and priorities. Without words, your classroom appearance contributes to the perception students initially form of you and telegraphs your brand. In this chapter, we look at ways to curate your classroom environment for optimal learning and comfort, to engage your students using the environment, and develop community with your students by learning more about them.

Be Aware of Your Classroom Environment

Although classroom environments vary across grade levels, some consistencies can help support students and make the classroom a welcoming place. Flexible seating is one example. An organized room should have makerspaces for group, collaborative, and independent learning built into its configuration. Providing flexible seating promotes learning because "changing spaces can make new ways of working and new perspectives visible" (Reinius, Korhonen, & Hakkarainen, 2021). Why not start our students out early with such possibilities? I have observed adults, more than ever, taking advantage of self-created workspaces in restaurants, airports, and coffee shops to work alone or in small groups. We should prepare students for the future by allowing them access to similar seating. In my classroom, I saw success in the flexible model in action. There were at least three areas with smaller tables or counter areas. These spaces were officially for small groups, but I also encouraged individual students to move to those areas while working. Allowing for seat choices created a sense of independence and, for some, a more productive place to work collaboratively and develop relationships. For the middle of the room, I arranged the desks in groups of three, four, five, or six desks and chairs for assorted seating. Then, I had a few of what I called "café seating," or a group of two. Students loved that one. It is important to note that I monitored the room closely as they worked independently and had very few issues with behavior. Every teacher is different, as is every classroom. You will find what works best for you. As you consider arrangements, think of the following questions about your room's flow and how you and your students will move.

- Where will students' materials be placed for easy access?
- Are resources positioned to prevent gridlock when students approach and use them? When resources are easily accessible, it is easier to monitor students' progress and assist them with their work.
- Where will you teach your lessons? I loved the interactive whiteboard but was not glued to the space in front of it. I especially enjoyed walking among the students as I taught to keep them more engaged and support my goal of interacting as we learned together.
- Have you adjusted for students who may have valid preferences? Do not assume you have. It may be wise to have a private conversation with a student (or parent) if you suspect strong preferences for seating. Remember that for various reasons, some personalities do not do well when seated near each other.

Furniture Arrangement

Students with documented special needs may require designated seat placement or access to certain room areas, including a student with an IEP (Individualized Education Plan), a 504 (a plan that ensures a student with a disability receives accommodations), a GIEP (Gifted Individualized Education Plan), or an OHI (Other Health Impaired). Chances are there will also be students with undocumented needs not yet identified who may need special seating. Sometimes, students go through troubling emotional times and require special consideration too. Feedback from former teachers, counselors, and parents may help you determine the best seating for those needing accommodations. Even a private conversation with the student can be fruitful. It is simple. Just ask them where they prefer to sit to learn the best. I have found students to be mostly honest with that question and seem appreciative. Another suggestion is to allow students to express their thoughts on classroom seating more definitively by using an online survey for immediate results or a paper version. Ask questions such as:

- If you could sit anywhere in the classroom, where would that be?
- What classroom seating arrangement makes you feel the most comfortable?
- Is it easier to see the board from up close or farther away?
- What other ideas do you have about seating that I should know?

Ensure you review all legal documents and personal circumstances to make the accommodations accordingly. Take time to consider the needs of every student. And, of course, arrangements can change as needed.

Classroom Décor

There are universal guidelines for classroom décor. One is cultural responsiveness, which provides cultural representation to help all students connect to the room and you. This can differ by student level and school locale, but one strategy is to post inclusive motivational quotes and posters that honor differences. It is essential to give students opportunities to construct and display depictions of their own cultures as they learn about the backgrounds of others.

Don't be nervous about making mistakes or misinterpreting what students may prefer. One August, when my district began the teaching year with multiple professional development days, there was less time than usual to set up classrooms. I put an "under construction" yellow ribbon on two bulletin boards with a sign reading, "Space for future student work." It was not my first choice, but necessity called for ingenuity. The students loved it! They were encouraged to know they had a place just for them, and we turned these bulletin boards into "cultural corners." I learned that what I may think is the most fantastic décor for walls and bulletin boards is not always what serves students in the best way.

Although numerous ideas are available for decorating and arranging your room, there are several agreed-on tips to keep in mind. If your room has too many reminders and rules, it may shout dictatorial rather than friendly. Color is good, but not in excessive amounts. Some students, such as those with autism spectrum disorders, do not do well with excessive stimuli as it may cause sensory overload and changes in behavior. Instead, a calming environment may work best for them (Chung & Son, 2020).

On the other hand, make sure your classroom content is not so limited that it looks cold. The best advice is to plan and decorate your room in moderation. In this way, you have a better chance of reaching more of your students.

Your classroom is a silent but powerful extension of you. Consider what you want to convey to your students when choosing your room's layout and makeup. Providing a warm, inviting environment is the foundation on which you will build your relationships, starting on the first day of school and then over time as you cultivate a classroom community of learners.

Engage Your Students

Today, teachers compete for student time and attention with an explosion of extracurricular activities, video games, and social media. Therefore, we cannot expect to reach today's students as teachers have in the past. We must rethink how we teach so we do not become an audience of one. It is vital to provide the engagement students crave, capture their attention, and, while doing so, allow ourselves fluidity in planning and implementation. Captivating student interest can be a catalyst in forming bonds with them.

Educators Allison Zmuda, Greg Curtis, and Diane Ullman (2015) recommend a student-driven learning model to engage students that is similar to inquiry-based learning but more structured. It incorporates three key areas. The first area is students *shift* when they have access to a variety of areas around the school itself. This concept is similar to flexible grouping by utilizing the classroom set-up idea of providing makerspaces and extending the idea to other areas around the school. The logistics of offering other spaces and assistance within the school campus may be limited where you are, but if not, check with the librarian, paraprofessionals, or special education teachers to see who can help. Meeting the needs of all students and providing the best environment for learning is where students may flourish the best. The second area is students *connect* through real-life experiences such as virtual and physical field trips and community outreach activities. An excellent example is using virtual technology to link learning to something more tangible. I had a family member who was studying in Paris. Studying the French culture was part of our classroom curriculum at the time. I had students write questions for her, and we videoconferenced so she could interact with the students and answer their queries. It turned out to be a powerful learning experience for them. You could also set up a virtual meeting with an author if you teach reading or English, a scientist or explorer for subjects like geography or biology, or an engineer for science or mathematics. You may need to research and plan, but once in place, it can also be something you can use in the future. At the very least, tying a lesson to world events can create a real-life simulation and lasting learning impression. For community outreach experiences, contact local nonprofit organizations and your township or county offices for student opportunities that coincide with your learning. The third area is students *navigate* goals and resources to promote more independent learning. This means providing technological opportunities for learning where students are encouraged to think more analytically and reflectively. An example is when a flipped classroom model is implemented, helping facilitate a more independent approach to learning. Students learn information on their own time, mostly outside of school for homework, and bring it to class where they have more time to develop and use higher-level thinking skills (We Are Teachers Staff, 2023).

Other noted educators have provided valuable models. In 1981, Kentucky educator Alice Johnson coined the phrase "a guide on the side, rather than a sage on the stage," referring to a new program for gifted and talented students (Aviles, 2018). Since that time, her words have become a mantra in many educational writings and practices. Educator and speaker Chris Aviles (2018) applied Johnson's prophetic words to the 21st century, asserting we should go beyond the "guide on the side" and morph into the COO, or chief opportunity orchestrator. He challenged teachers to provide opportunities for students by creating what he calls "dare to be great moments" (Aviles, 2018). This is where you think creatively to develop memory-worthy learning experiences with and for students.

One of the schools where I taught has an involved project where students collaborate in groups to design a product and create a business plan to market it, including developing financials and simulating sales. Experiences like these allow students to be connected, involved, and *actively* engaged. These two kinds of engagement are quite different: being involved is going through the motions and simply participating. Being actively engaged is being absorbed and having a thirst for more. Use the following prompt to reflect on previous experiences with active engagement.

Think about some experiences of active engagement you have either witnessed or facilitated. What "dare to be great" moments come to mind?

Purposeful and Positive Goal Setting

The benefits of establishing yourself as an encouraging, compassionate, and innovative educator are boundless. In your quest to make connections, you can open students' minds and allow them to learn enthusiastically. How you present yourself can influence the quality of your classroom and make students more open to getting to know you. As the COO of your classroom, set and practice personal goals and outcomes that can help you focus on developing an enlightened classroom—with the use of purposeful "if-then" scenarios. Some examples include:

- If you show enthusiasm, your students will be more enthused.
- If you show confidence, your students will demonstrate self-efficacy.
- If you are nonjudgmental, your students will feel more accepted.

If-then statements are formally called *implementation intentions*. These words speak for themselves: set your objectives and carry them out. Peter M. Gollwitzer (1999) concluded that implementation intentions are beneficial in realizing desired outcomes, and repeated intentions can become habitual, leading to goal automaticity. There is a degree of flexibility and grace as your target could end up being missed, but the opportunity to try again or reset the goal is possible. Make sure your goals are realistic. "Implementation intentions are a powerful tool that can facilitate goal striving, but they must be formed thoughtfully" (Parks-Stamm & Gollwitzer, 2009, p. 386). In other words, one should carefully consider the if-then statement's efficacy when planning. Is it substantial enough? Does it make sense? Being intentional about what we wish to change in ourselves or how we act can lead students to see more of the best we have to offer as educators.

Try formulating some helpful or encouraging goals you could establish with your students. Use the following prompt box to record any that come to mind.

Think about and list a few if-then statements of your own.

Connecting with students means meeting them at their level and discovering what makes them tick. What are their general ideas about home, school, peers, activities, colleagues, and school? The more we know our students, the more we can precisely address each of their needs. With this approach, we can avoid the attitude and discipline issues that can arise from making (often incorrect) assumptions.

One year, I sensed a student severely lacked a sense of belonging. I made a sincere effort to engage him and give him the necessary attention. However, this student required more individual attention than I was providing. He felt left out, even though I often gave him even more attention than others. This made my heart sink. Could I have taken it personally and chosen to dig in my heels? Yes, of course. However, I knew from experience that to change a student's perspective and make them feel part of the class, I needed to find the root cause. Through conversation, I found out that his mother was physically, but not mentally, present in his life. This student craved attention to fill the void. After learning this, I was able to convince him to speak to our counselor. However, my involvement did not end there. I ensured he felt appreciated and accepted each day, not in a phony way, but in a genuine manner. Small gestures seemed to work, such as offering an extra smile, choosing him to run an errand, and empowering him to help other students.

Another student became visibly upset whenever I asked her for missing assignments, even when I asked privately to avoid embarrassing her in front of her peers. The problem? The student was not lazy or negligent. She simply needed help with time management. Although she did not have an Individualized Education Plan, I helped her plan and organize tasks to visualize dates and times. As we worked on this together, it made all the difference.

I am happy these circumstances did not happen often, but they are examples of learning experiences that are wonderfully serendipitous. They are reminders that specifically targeted relationship building is necessary, even if you must make a U-turn and return because of a missed opportunity. We had a motto at my school: *Whatever it takes*. These simple and powerful words can keep us focused on establishing a winning relationship with our students leading to student success—emotionally, behaviorally, and academically.

Find Out About Your Students

Early in the school year, teachers sometimes give their students interest inventories to get to know them better. These are typically a set of questions designed to encourage students to open up about their likes and sometimes, their dislikes. So, what information is most pertinent for a teacher to know? I believe it is up to each teacher. If you are an art teacher, you may want to learn whether students prefer classical or modern art and whether they are familiar with art history. As a reading teacher, you may want to tailor your questions in the form of a reading inventory to see what students have read and where their reading interests lie. Use the following prompt to discover your own unique questions to ask students to try to know them better.

What do you want to know about your students that will help inform you and help meet their needs at their level? List some of your ideas.

You probably produced some outstanding questions you could ask your students. Take another look and see if any are "fluff" questions. For example, do you really need to know their favorite color or most-liked food? Eliminate questions that do not dig deeper into their interests and background. The following are some ideas for questions of value. Other information, such as favorite colors, will come naturally later. One final note: be sure not to overwhelm your students. A few questions a day at the beginning of the year is more than enough, especially for younger ages. For older students, adding space for optional additional comments can be helpful. You can find a printable reproducible of these questions at the end of the chapter (page 53).

- When is your birthday or another special day that celebrates just you? (This makes one feel valued.)
- Do you have a nickname? (Again, it makes them feel valued, and it is crucial to call students by the name they desire and with correct pronunciation to not only show respect but also to avoid embarrassing them in front of classmates.)
- Are there any other young people in your family? (With blended or extended families, the word *sibling* may not be appropriate.)
- Describe an enjoyable memory. (This is a good starting point for an individual conversation later.)
- What do you like to do outside of school? (This is another starting point for an individual conversation.)
- How do you like to work in class? (Circle one)
    - By myself
    - With a partner
    - In a group
- How do you like your teacher to communicate with you? (Circle all that apply)
    - In front of everyone
    - Quietly on the side
    - By email
- How do you feel about your success in school? (Circle one)
    - Great!
    - OK
    - Not so good

Again, these are just examples. During the first days of the year, you will want to focus on the essential information about your students. When you read about the planning piece of establishing a relationship in an upcoming chapter, this knowledge gathering will be one of your first steps.

Practice Empathy With Your Students

There is incredible power in creating an empathetic classroom. Empathy is understanding and connecting with others emotionally. In a study with student participants on the topic of discipline, researchers concluded that an "empathic mindset" as opposed to a "punitive mindset" was more conducive to improving behaviors and engagement (Okonofua, Paunesku, & Walton, 2016). Furthermore, findings also stated that more positive mental attitude changes require practicing and refining to be effective. One of my colleagues drives this theory home through a class community service model. She is active in nonprofit organizations and has traveled often to Africa for service work. I have always admired her focus on outreach, and she has passed this along to her students. Her class has organized several service projects, including collecting canned goods for shelters, creating placemats and other gifts for nursing home residents, and fundraising for those in need. She teaches her students the joy of putting others before themselves by showing them what it means to help others unconditionally. As they participate in philanthropic activities, students grow closer as a class, helping to produce open-mindedness to learning. Also, using the theme-based approach, she integrates all disciplines—mathematics, history, research, and more—into the service activity at hand. Her approach is summed up in this quote (falsely attributed to Aristotle): "Educating the mind without educating the heart is no education at all" (Sententiae Antiquae, 2017). Her methods were unconventional and classroom community service worked for her. However, it may not be for everyone. Any service activity should be authentic and meaningful to the teacher for students to buy in and appreciate its benefits. Learning individual student voices and learning to practice respect for your students are the cornerstones of having empathy for students.

Your Students' Voices

One of the best ways to create a strong classroom community is to give students a voice in their learning. As mentioned earlier, one way to do this is by enhancing the classroom by displaying expressions of students' work. Don't forget that their work can be displayed elsewhere, such as your school website, newsletters, hallways, or other district platforms. Encouraging students to choose what work they wish to display is another way to give them a voice and believe more in themselves. There is something powerful about a student making decisions instead of going along with what the teacher thinks.

Beyond giving students choices, I recommend involving them in the planning process. For example, suppose you are planning a new unit. Pre-assessing your students' knowledge is helpful, but what if you go one step further and ask them if they have ideas of how they could best learn the upcoming unit's content? You might be surprised by the responses and find avenues for learning you hadn't considered. Then, if student ideas are implemented, there is empowerment and subsequent buy-in.

Another method of empowering students is modeling humility. Beginning on the first day, I stressed that we were a community of learners. I admitted that I did not know everything, and we would seek answers together if we had questions or were curious about any subjects. It worked! Every day, there was a question about what we were learning or another topic. Together we would take a few minutes to research the answer. (Of course, it helps if there is access to at least one classroom computer.)

I adopted my "together we can learn" attitude years ago when I observed a student teacher who would set up a hunt for answers and then create exciting tidbits to "pop" the lesson and engage the students. It was a form of tag-teaming, and students loved it. They jumped on board, learning became an active group effort, and they solidified their community of learners. Students were comfortable taking risks in class, and their active involvement created a thirst for knowledge.

Respect for Your Students

Under the umbrella of people skills lies the essential component of respect. Unfortunately, it is not something that comes naturally to everyone. Preservice teachers, beginning teachers, and even some experienced teachers may desperately need resources or training to learn and grow relationally (Farhah, Saleh, & Safitri, 2021). When respect is understood, practiced, and makes its way into the classroom, students can feel its tangible presence. Listening with intent, showing compassion, and acknowledging unique identities make students feel recognized and respected. Fostering respect in the classroom between you and your students and between students and their peers adds to the quality and overall ease of relationship building.

It has been an honor to have collaborated with many outstanding teachers who have been excellent role models and provided terrific philosophies.

One such teacher was the gifted resource teacher for the school where I taught fifth grade. He had a respectful way of managing a classroom that was quite simple yet highly effective. He had a method called the *courtesy warning*. If a student talked while he was speaking, he would lean down and whisper "courtesy warning" while not missing a beat of instruction. Students knew this was the warning before the consequence and understood not to continue talking. His respect for his students was returned in their respect for him. I often used the same method. It worked wonderfully because it avoided calling out the specifics of the behavior. Even though he removed a few students over the years who crossed the line, overall, using this kind of respectful disciplinary strategy in the classroom was a beautiful thing and contributed to building the classroom community.

The courtesy warning is just one example of how you can weave respect throughout your classroom. Another way is to make sure you have time for the questions and concerns of each student. At times, it can seem like an impossible feat. If a student needs immediate attention, you need to make yourself available. However, it is OK to tell students who need nonurgent assistance that you will circle back and take care of them. Once you have shaped a respectful classroom, most students will be content to wait if you have acknowledged them.

I gently caution you to be mindful of what you say and how you say it to any student in front of their peers. Communicating with a student should be as discreet as possible unless you are 100 percent certain you will not offend them in front of others. Be sure to know them well before making remarks they may misconstrue or assume they are OK with joking around. I realize this is common sense, but having seen colleagues embarrass students without thinking, it is essential to note. Remember, it is not just that one student might feel singled out because of an embarrassing remark or action; other students may feel empathy for them too.

Conclusion

At the beginning of the year, consider the students' perspectives when envisioning your classroom look and feel. What do they see within your room and how does it communicate to them? What emotions do you want them to see and feel? What questions or assumptions might they have about you as a person and as an educator? Do they predict an inclusive environment with respect where students are valued? Besides your morning greeting and body language, your space will also write volumes on your behalf. Students will begin to make connections with you as they identify with the contents of the room. Giving some thought to their judgment of your room plays a part in beginning a relationship with them, and you want to start in a positive light.

Kick off the year with some experiences that are planned and ready to implement. Some ideas might include inquiry-based learning choices, real-life options, collaborative settings, and student-led learning. Engaging opportunities will make students love coming to your class each day and help in forging bonds.

As you take the time to learn more about your students, you can create an atmosphere of respect. Encourage empathic responses as you set an example for understanding, humility, acceptance, and compassion. Once students begin to feel a sense of belonging in the environment you establish, it will be much easier for you to cultivate meaningful connections with them.

The goal is to create a solid classroom community where one feels safe, welcome, and has a sense of belonging without alienation. Helping students improve how they think about themselves removes roadblocks in the learning process. In this chapter, there are several key ideas to help you, but in no way is it an exhaustive list. Take what you can use and keep exploring more ways to develop a strong learning community in your classroom as you build bonds.

Questions to Get to Know Your Students

- When is your birthday or another special day that celebrates just you? (This makes one feel valued.)

- Do you have a nickname? (Again, this makes them feel valued, and it is crucial to call students by the name they desire and with correct pronunciation to not only show respect but also to avoid embarrassing them in front of classmates.)

- Are there any other young people in your family? (With blended or extended families, the word *sibling* may not be appropriate.)

- Describe an enjoyable memory. (This is a good starting point for an individual conversation later.)

- What do you like to do outside of school? (This is another starting point for an individual conversation.)

- How do you like to work in class? (Circle one)

  By myself   With a partner   In a group

- How do you like your teacher to communicate with you? (Circle all that apply)

In front of everyone   Quietly on the side   By email

- How do you feel about your success in school? (Circle one)

  Great!   OK   Not so good

4

Build Your Communication

Communication is the most important skill in life. We spend most of our waking hours communicating. But consider this: You've spent years learning how to read and write, years learning how to speak. But what about listening? What training or education have you had that enables you to listen so that you really, deeply understand another human being from that individual's own frame of reference?

—Stephen R. Covey

I learned much of what I can tell you about communication from experience. I do not recall being explicitly taught how to interact with students, parents, colleagues, or administrators. It was something that seemed to grow organically through time and experience. Fortunately, I paid attention to other teachers who were communication experts. Early on, those brilliant mentors helped me navigate the education highway much better than if I had gone solo.

Some educators have an easy time communicating, whether in person or electronically, one-to-one or in groups, verbally or in writing. They seem to circumvent all obstacles and smoothly create beneficial relationships. However, if you struggle, take heart. Interacting appropriately and consistently calls for reflecting and then adapting—in other words, learning. It is important to admit when things don't quite go as well as you had hoped because mistakes can build common sense and skill. However, this is the most challenging piece to accept. When things may have gone differently, taking the high road may not be the easy way out, but it is the best way to mend a relationship or, at the very least, avoid damaging it further.

Especially in our profession, I cannot stress enough the importance of effective communication. Whether you interact in person or electronically via email, text, or video conference, the basic protocol is to be respectful and kind—no matter what. Sadly, misinterpretations can happen. Just as gestures can escalate emotions, choosing the wrong words, using the wrong tone, or lacking clarity can derail your intentions and cause relationship discord. If you find yourself in these situations, whenever possible, have confidence that all is not lost. Pull your conversation back into a positive light. In this chapter, you'll learn how to effectively practice listening; set discussion goals to keep you focused on your interactions; communicate with students, colleagues, and staff; redirect a conversational path when it strays; and adapt these practices to conversations between educators and students, parents, and peers.

Learn From Your Communication Experiences

Communication can build or break relationships and make the difference between a fantastic or horrific year. I had one of those years. It was perfect until the last conference of the year when I dug in my heels about a report card grade the parent felt their child did not deserve, even though the student clearly did not earn the higher grade. She felt her child was never a "C student" and did not deserve the grade I *gave* to him. Calmly, I told her he had *earned* the "C" and showed her some of his work to support my claim. She became angry and raised her voice. Even though she should have noticed his graded assignments, tests, quizzes, and the mid-marking period progress report, along with the online scores, she felt it was my responsibility to let her know his grade was below a "B." Amidst the heated discussion, I realized there was more basis to her anger than originally thought. Her son would not qualify for the year-end honor roll award for all four marking periods. I tried to remain calm and did not back down. Unfortunately, the remainder of the meeting was a volley of her insistence and my lack of surrender. In the end, the "C" remained. The once amicable relationship between mother and son had dissolved. What did I learn? Many things. First, I learned to be more prepared for specific conferences. I had been given a heads-up that the parents were unhappy but didn't adequately consider how the meeting might pan out. When I saw his grade slip toward the end of the marking period, I could have emailed the parent or offered extra credit to all students to possibly help their grades. Second, I realized that it is OK to table a conversation by acknowledging the concern and offering to reanalyze the grade for accuracy. Sometimes, it may be best to try and reschedule for another time to better prepare. When it comes to difficult discussions, twenty minutes of conference time is never enough, especially when the conversation becomes heated. Third, I discovered that bringing the student and an administrator into the conversation can be helpful. In hindsight, it would have been better to have my principal and the student attend the conference to ensure a more peaceful and productive conversation. I have had several students who struggled with severe academic or behavioral issues. With these students, it was always beneficial to have the student, any support staff, and the administrator in the meeting because it formed a respectful gathering of *all* minds. In all honestly, it sometimes made students feel uneasy with so many adults in a meeting. However, once they understood we were their team to help them, it seemed to make them feel they were worthy and not alone.

Finally, and perhaps most importantly, I learned that we must give the benefit of the doubt to those with whom we communicate. About fifteen years after that awful parent meeting, I learned there had been struggles at home that may have contributed to our communication disconnect. Thankfully, it was the last exchange where I experienced such anger. Moving forward, I learned to visualize how each conference would go and I made sure that I was better prepared with background information on each student. I considered whether any support personnel or administrator should be present. Also, prior to the conferences, I sent a confirmation home to each parent or guardian along with a prompt soliciting any questions they had. Most parents sent back responses, even if it was merely confirming their attendance. Making time to research and think about any concerns parents or guardians had *before* our meeting helped me to be more organized, gave me added confidence, and produced a profound sense of peace for me.

Thoughtful, respectful, and positive communication is essential in cultivating solid and productive relationships with all stakeholders, with the key benefit of enhancing your students' experiences and learning. It also becomes part of your brand, as we discussed. Moreover, thorough communication benefits your career, and who does not want to be successful? The following section details the various kinds of communication you can put into practice to become an effective communicator and listener.

Identify Different Kinds of Communication

The importance of teacher communication cannot be overemphasized. It is a critical piece in building relationships with students, parents, and administrators (Salamondra, 2021). The following content is broken down into organized categories and features useful ways to communicate with educational constituents. First, we begin with one of the largest parts of mindful and effective communication: *listening* (Rodat, 2019).

Listening

Listening skills, especially *active* listening, are something that must be taught. Yet, to focus on preservice education and professional development repertoire is limited compared to verbal instruction (Spataro & Bloch, 2017). I honestly cannot remember an undergraduate or graduate course or professional development module strictly devoted to learning teacher listening skills. I thought of communication as merely spoken words. It makes sense that listening is integral; you need both a speaker and a listener to converse.

The key components of listening are casual and engaged. A casual listener hears what is being said and may act on what is heard and respond. However, an engaged listener is considered an active listener. They may do so by using body language such as facial expressions, nodding their head in agreement while listening, or commenting with short words to show the speaker they are taking in the conversation. This type of listener will appear focused, allowing the speaker to finish without interruption, and they may ask questions or summarize what was said (Rodat, 2019). You can recognize someone when they are entirely immersed in the conversation because of the intentional way they are listening. Hopefully, you can see how learning about listening and striving to be an effective communicator is congruent with establishing student relationships.

General Communication Etiquette

The following pieces of advice represent a handful of common sense guidelines that are most important for educators. All of them, in their own way, contribute to building bonds with students. Communication with parents, colleagues, and administrators are discussed since they can be influential in establishing relationships with students.

- *Respond to verbal or written communication on the same day, or at least within 24 hours.* This is a guideline in my school district. One time, I was out sick for several days. A parent had left a message on the first day I was out. By the time I returned to school, I had received an unpleasant email from him and was berated for not responding promptly. After our conversation, all was well. I learned that students do not always tell their parents when you are out of the classroom. If you can, it would be advantageous to turn on an automatic out-of-the-office response on your email alerting all who try to contact you. For extended leaves when you are going to be out, a mass email or note home could be sent. It is courteous and may help you avoid an uncomfortable encounter.

- *Take negative emotions out.* Preemptively write what you want to say on a separate document. Then, take the high road in your actual communication. Do not write it in an email text box because you could inadvertently send it. I have found great success in acknowledging the receiver's perspective first and then expressing what I need to say. I gained this knowledge after my experience with the "C" grade parent conference debacle, mentioned earlier. Human nature appreciates being heard.
- *Try not to take it personally if anyone is upset.* Our counselor had a unique visual way of spelling this idea out for students and teachers. She advised us to QTIP: Quit Taking It Personally. People have bad days and sometimes they may transfer their feelings onto you. If you receive a heated email, it may be best to wait to respond until after you have had time to consider their intentions carefully and formulate a professional response. My colleagues and I consistently ran emails by one another to check for tone or attitude adjustments.
- *Use the sandwich technique, whether the communication is verbal or nonverbal.* Begin with positive comments, follow with any constructive criticism, and end with another positive remark. For example, Johnny may struggle academically so you could start by saying he is creative and cooperative when working with peers. He needs to stay focused during lessons because it will help him to improve his grades. Lastly, mention something about his character that is special such as his willingness to help clean up the classroom or his undeniable humor (Prochazka, Ovcari, & Durinik, 2020). If you can embellish these layers, that is even

better. In conferences with multiple colleagues, I saw the faces of parents sour when they heard too many negative comments about their child and not enough positivity. The sandwich technique is a good rule for students, colleagues, families, or administrators.

- *Keep your responses short, sweet, and straightforward while conveying a positive vibe.* Staying focused on what you want to say keeps you from sounding wishy-washy or unintelligent. Weed out unnecessary verbiage. You will lessen your chances of the recipient misunderstanding your message and increase their chances of reading the entire email. Researchers have found that the optimum average range is between 25–60 words per email (Altamimi et al., 2020). Readers should not have to guess what you are trying to convey. With your fingers poised on the keyboard, think first about the purpose of your email, organize your thoughts, and be succinct as you write. Your message should be easily understood. For longer conversations and sensitive information, call to discuss or schedule a meeting.
- *Content should be professional.* Unless you know the person to whom you are writing well, project a more business-like approach without coming across as abrupt or frosty. With school emails, I have tried to write them so anyone in the world can read them without being offended. This is especially true with personal information. Check your district's policies. They may require you to refrain from mentioning student names or personal information. In addition, check your state for public records laws and regulations as they vary nationwide (National Conference of State Legislatures, 2023).
- *Be clear, concise, careful, and considerate.* Try to prioritize what you want to say from most important to least. Your words can be misconstrued more online than when you express yourself verbally. Keep in mind that anyone, at any time, can see your email once it is sent. I have known a couple of teachers in my career who took great pride in writing copious emails to parents with concerns. Their efforts initiated a volleying of responses back and forth, often ending up with a phone call for clarification. Greetings and closings are excellent spots to show your individual style and smile.
- *State your purpose.* When crafting your email, write the purpose in the subject line. This is helpful for the recipient to know upfront

what your email contains and assists them in sorting and saving emails as a reference.

- *Avoid possible embarrassment.* Avoid what Victoria Turk (2019) calls *reply-apocalypse.* This is when you hit "reply-all" instead of your intended reply to one individual. It can start a chain of subsequent reply-all responses and become humiliating. I saw that happen at least once a week at my school. Over time, I witnessed a few sensitive emails, and it was not a good look for the senders, believe me.

Recalling your focus on building relationships every time you communicate can help you avoid uncomfortable situations. Following practical wisdom for communicating with colleagues, administrators, parents, and students can help you draft professional emails and speak professionally with others without sacrificing your individual personality. The good news is you can still be professionally proficient and genuine at the same time.

Online Communication

Stepping into the cyberspace arena can be tricky, especially for educators since the professional bar is set high. What you post online can be available to the public for years to come unless it is deleted from the server you are using. In the following paragraphs, you will find guidelines to help you with cyber integrity to keep your reputation safe.

- *Avoid any social media your district or school does not support.* Just because you may not have had training on the subject does not mean you are exonerated from any liability with online communication. Even if district or school policy does not specify staying off social platforms, you still need to protect your image. Like it or not, you are judged on what you post and what others may contribute to that post. I suggest referring to the book *Emily Post's Manners in a Digital World: Living Well Online* (Senning, 2013). It is an entire book dedicated to how to navigate and protect yourself in cyberspace.
- *Respect FERPA.* That is the Family Educational Rights and Privacy Act. It is a law to protect student privacy. Be careful about what you include in your emails. Visit www2.ed.gov/policy/gen/guid/fpco/ferpa/index.html to review the FERPA regulations.

- *Maximize your communication.* If your school has a platform for online learning, use it to its full extent with parents and students. Posting homework, coursework, daily activities, and nonconfidential information can strengthen involvement.
- *Use a "trifecta" approach.* For example, if you post information online, it might not be seen if accessing the site is complicated or if technology is nonexistent at home. A hard copy may not make it out of the backpack and students may not be consistent with logging important notes into their assignment book either. I suggest covering yourself and ensuring that information, whether it is homework, an assignment, or other school communication, is available through three avenues. This can dodge possible nasty responses.
- *Watch grammar and spelling.* For formal or semiformal writing, grammar rules should be applied, with the exception being when you communicate with a close friend. Use capitals at the beginning of sentences but avoid typing in all caps as it may come across as shouting and impolite. Instead, try italicizing or underlining any word or words you want to stand out. Ensure you use accurate punctuation and sentence structure (The Editorial Team, 2020). You are an educator and, like it or not, you could be judged by your lack of careful attention to your online voice.
- *Stay current.* Once you create a website, keep it up to date. It can be frustrating to others if outdated. That applies to posting grades if your school has an online grading system as well (Dyches, Carter, & Prater, 2012). As a side note, remember it is important to be sensitive to families who do not have access to the internet.

Mandated Reporting

Mandated reporting is another rare form of communication that can affect our relationships with students. This is a legal requirement for teachers to report any suspected neglect or abuse of a minor. Teachers are not alone. Many individuals, including those in the medical field, are obligated to report. The following are key points to examine. I encourage you to research the state requirements where you teach to increase your knowledge base.

- Whether you have received training in reporting suspected abuse or not, it is your responsibility to be aware. Check with your state and district guidelines in advance to make sure you understand the entire reporting protocol.

- The website www.childwelfare.gov provides information about mandated reporting and links to state resources.
- It can be challenging for a minor to come forward and disclose to you they have been abused or neglected. The more a student trusts you, the more they will choose the risk of telling you over possible consequences from a perpetrator.
- The law is the law. If your state requires mandated reporting, you *must* act, regardless of whether you feel conflicted or may breach a student's trust. It may seem like the antithesis of building a positive relationship, but you need to consider what is in the best interest of each child.

Allow me to explain this last bullet point in more detail. It is our obligation as professional educators to report any suspected abuse to Child Protective Services and failure to do so can result in penalties (Child Welfare Information Gateway, 2019). This can be frightening. Trust me. I have been there. To avoid angst when reporting, I have found it helpful to reach out to the school counselor or administration with suspected child abuse or neglect, especially if I was not sure whether an incident needed to be reported or not. I know of colleagues who hesitated to become involved because they feared retribution. It can be human nature to feel scared about the unknown. However, we need to consider that when we do report, we are protected. In all fifty states, reporters are granted immunity from "civil or criminal liability" (Child Welfare Information Gateway, 2023). I urge you to check with your state for clarification and specific statutes. Forewarned is forearmed.

Educator to Parent or Guardian Communication

In our efforts to shape great relationships with students, teachers as well as students and parents or guardians need to be on the same page, working together as a team, and in the best interest of the child. This requires going beyond an occasional note home or a general mass email. Instead, intentionally calling home to report positives instead of issues is more conducive to growing solid relationships with students and those who support them outside of school (Kraft & Dougherty, 2013). This is not a new concept, but one that is not so easy due to the demands of the profession. Chunk your time by reaching out to one or two parents a day and recording your interactions with them. For teachers in secondary schools where class sizes are larger than elementary, you may want to focus on what we used to call the "highfliers." They were the students on our radar for behavioral or academic reasons. Using a parent-teacher logbook is helpful. They can be purchased, or you can simply use a composition notebook. Toward the end of this book, there will be more discussion on how to organize your communication efforts.

As you read the following communication suggestions, think about how you might use them in your classroom.

- If a parent or caregiver sends a heated email, ask them when a good time would be to reach them by phone. In my experience, speaking over the telephone or in person helps avoid any misconceptions that an email or text can inadvertently create.
- Choose a handful of students each week and reach out to their families with a positive note or email. Make it short and sincere. The amount of time this takes will more than pay out with how much it can enhance your relations with students and their families.
- Send verbal praise home with your students. I began this idea early in my career and it worked well most of the time. When complimenting a student, ask them to repeat what you said at home. It is another way to send positive comments home.
- Use technology where permissible. Websites like www.remind.com can help communicate with parents and help students meet their educational goals. There are many online communication tools, but make sure your district sanctions them before use. And, of course, do not unfairly leave out students who do not have technology at home.
- Acknowledge a concern or question even if you don't have time to address it at that moment. If a parent emails, send a quick reply to let them know when you will respond in detail. Then, make sure you follow through.
- Use email when necessary. Some examples are a quick reply, schedule, or if you need documentation showing you have advised the parent or guardian. Do not send confidential documents

(student or otherwise), anything private, or a forwarded email from someone without their permission (Dyches et al., 2012).

Educator to Student Communication

Some ideas I learned throughout my career may be helpful for you in strengthening your communication and relationships with students. I gave them to substitute teachers when I was not present and shared them with interested colleagues.

- *Make sure you communicate with your students respectfully, including pulling them aside privately so others cannot hear.* Young people can become embarrassed easily. What seemed to always work for me was to find a quiet time, like during transitioning to lunch or another class. The worst thing you could do as a teacher is speak to a student in class while all their peers are listening. There are those rare students who are so confident in themselves that speaking with them in front of others is not an issue, but you must be sure it is comfortable for them.
- *Be humble. Do not be afraid to say you were wrong.* Sometimes, it takes courage to admit when we make a mistake, but the effects can be far-reaching. This took me a while to learn, but the payoff in being honest was enormous. I recall a vivid experience when I pointed out to a student that she was cheating on an online quiz. It turned out to be a glitch in the computer system for the online quiz, and she was completely correct—she did not cheat. I acknowledged my mistake, and we remained on good terms.
- *Use journals as another way to communicate.* The first time I used a communication journal was when I returned to a short-term teaching assignment after my children were born. The beloved teacher I replaced was on maternity leave. I was told that I had big shoes to fill and some parents were worried about who was taking over in the interim. I had an idea as to how to ease parents' and students' concerns about not having the teacher they had grown to know over the previous seven months. I told the students they could write anything they wanted their teacher to know and that I would make sure she saw their comments. It worked beautifully. It made me realize that a small gesture could make a huge difference. I have continued to use this communication tool as a bridge between home and school with students who need support. I have also used it in the classroom by placing a journal in an area where

students have access to it. This allows them to write what they want you to know. It serves as a suggestion box. This is especially helpful with shy, reserved students.

- *If a student asks you a private question and you cannot answer at that time, set a time to circle back.* I have found that if you acknowledge students, they will generally wait. Keep in mind that it is best to let them know the approximate time you will be checking back with them.
- *Reaffirm that you are there to help.* Sometimes, students assume we are too busy. They see us constantly moving about according to the schedule at hand. Let them know often that you are a valuable resource for them. I had a student tell me once that she did not come to me sooner about the issue because she saw I was so busy. Reiterate to your students that you are there for them no matter what. Tell them to leave you a note if they think you are too involved in the workings of the day.
- *Keep a close eye on students' missing work.* A student-led check-in requirement acknowledging they have submitted work can quickly flag any missing assignments. Of course, an online platform for submitting work is efficient because it can pinpoint the submission date. However, use this only for students with technology at home. Have an independent check-in station set up in your room where students mark off if they have left their homework.
- *Use sticky notes to communicate reminders that show you care.* It is cathartic—good for the soul. Send positive notes throughout the year so that all students will feel included. Notes can be used to set up a time to meet with those who may be on the shy or introverted side. Have fun with it!

Educator to Administration Communication

The significance of engaging your administrative team deserves serious real estate in this section. I am not just talking about communicating with them for personnel-type needs like a day off (although that is important). Your principal, assistant principal, psychologist, social worker, counselor, learning support teachers, and administrative secretaries are there for you. Please do not forget that. We must pull together all adult resources and remember we are not on an island, alone, with our students.

I have tapped the brain of our counselor numerous times. She was generously forthcoming with ideas for hard-to-reach students. When you are trying to connect with some students, they can put up a wall. Counselors are trained to understand how to break through to these students. Use their knowledge. Counselors are often willing to be partners in forging relationships with students.

Principals are mentors. Keep them in the loop. I had a withdrawn student who lacked home support and needed recognition, so I asked our administrator to acknowledge the student privately. Our administrator stopped him in the hallway to say, "I hear you did an incredible job on your recent project." His face lit up. One statement and miles of self-esteem were created that day. This scenario could be done by any of the administrative team members. Do not discount them. Another principal was appreciative of my heads-up communication. Helicopter parents were prevalent in my school, and they seemed to vent to this principal regularly. I made sure I alerted her each time I had a parent conversation that might find its way to her office. By having a partnership, we averted the possibility of some uncomfortable situations.

Respect resonates and serves to help us in our endeavors with relationships. Hopefully, these examples of how the entire school community can support your efforts in strengthening relationships with your students will assist you too.

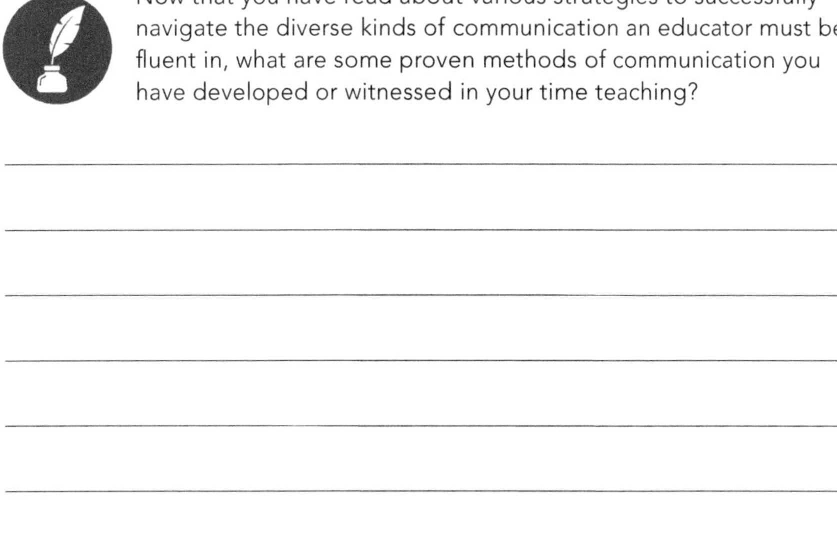

Now that you have read about various strategies to successfully navigate the diverse kinds of communication an educator must be fluent in, what are some proven methods of communication you have developed or witnessed in your time teaching?

Conclusion

In this chapter, you discovered information and tips on how to communicate with all stakeholders in an educational setting: support staff, parents, administrators, colleagues, or the students you teach each day. We looked at commonsense ways of approaching communication, via email, online, or in person. In addition, we discussed necessary steps to ensure that information found in student's education documents is kept discreet and secure.

At the end of the day, the communication you utilize at school and in your classroom makes the difference between a healthy, enjoyable career and one that feels tethered, forever blowing in the wind. With practice, communicating becomes easier. With time, the outcome can be priceless. In the next chapter, we will dive more deeply into the teacher-student relationship by focusing on relationship building with students with special needs. You will learn tips and wisdom from a seasoned teacher panel and evidence-based strategies for takeaways.

5

Support Your Students' Special Needs

See the able, not the label.
—Anonymous

Each year during my district's teacher in-service sessions, we dedicate time to focus on differentiation and meeting the needs of *all* students. During one memorable session, we were presented with a short story written by Jamie Vollmer, a former business executive and now an educational consultant, speaker, and public school advocate. His powerful tapestry of words is transcribed for you. Please take a moment to read it, reflect, and respond.

The Blueberry Story: The Teacher Gives the Businessman a Lesson

"If I ran my business the way you people operate your schools, I wouldn't be in business very long!"

I stood before an auditorium filled with outraged teachers who were becoming angrier by the minute. My speech had entirely consumed their precious 90 minutes of in-service. Their initial icy glares had turned to restless agitation. You could cut the hostility with a knife.

I represented a group of businesspeople dedicated to improving public schools. I was an executive at an ice cream company that became famous in the mid-1980s when **People Magazine** chose our blueberry as the "Best Ice Cream in America."

I was convinced of two things. First, public schools needed to change; they were archaic selecting and sorting mechanisms designed for the industrial age and out of step with the needs of our emerging "knowledge society." Second, educators were a major part of the problem: they resisted change, hunkered down in their feathered nests, protected by tenure, and shielded by a bureaucratic monopoly. They needed to look to business. We knew how to produce quality. Zero defects! TQM! Continuous improvement!

In retrospect, the speech was perfectly balanced—equal parts ignorance and arrogance.

As soon as I finished, a woman's hand shot up. She appeared polite, pleasant—she was, in fact, a razor-edged, veteran, high school English teacher who had been waiting to unload.

She began quietly, "We are told, Sir, that you manage a company that makes good ice cream."

I smugly replied, "Best ice cream in America, Ma'am."

"How nice," she said. "Is it rich and smooth?"

"Sixteen percent butterfat," I crowed.

"Premium ingredients?" she inquired.

"Super-premium! Nothing but triple A." I was on a roll. I never saw the next line coming.

"Mr. Vollmer," she said, leaning forward with a wicked eyebrow raised to the sky, "When you are standing on your receiving dock and you see an inferior shipment of blueberries arrive, what do you do?"

In the silence of that room, I could hear the trap snap. I was dead meat, but I wasn't going to lie.

"I send them back."

She jumped to her feet. "That's right!" she barked, "And we can never send back ***our*** blueberries. We take them big, small, rich, poor, gifted, exceptional, abused, frightened, confident, homeless, rude, and brilliant. We take them with ADHD, junior rheumatoid arthritis, and English as their second language. We take them all! Every one! And that, Mr. Vollmer, is why it's not a business. It's a school!"

In an explosion, all 290 teachers, principals, bus drivers, aides, custodians, and secretaries jumped to their feet and yelled, "Yeah! Blueberries! Blueberries!"

And so began my long transformation.

Since then, I have visited hundreds of schools. I have learned that a school is not a business. Schools are unable to control the quality of their raw material, they are dependent upon the vagaries of politics for a reliable revenue stream, and they are constantly mauled by a howling horde of disparate, competing customer groups that would send the best CEO screaming into the night.

None of this negates the need for change. We must change what, when, and how we teach to give all children the maximum opportunity to thrive in a post-industrial society. But educators cannot do this alone; these changes can occur only with the understanding, trust, permission, and active support of the surrounding community. The most important thing I have learned is that schools reflect the attitudes, beliefs, and health of the communities they serve, and therefore, to improve public education means more than changing our schools, it means changing America.

Jamie Robert Vollmer, © 2011.

Jamie Vollmer is a former business executive and attorney who now works to increase public support for America's public schools. For more information, visit www.SchoolsCannotDoItAlone.com

That's right. Blueberries. We take them all and, more than that, appreciate them all. No matter what background, behavior, academic, social, or emotional needs they may have. Special needs are unique to each individual and involve tailored support to ensure that students thrive and reach their full potential. They can include physical accommodations, such as wheelchair accessibility or hearing aids, as well as emotional and academic support like counseling or extra tutoring. Social support is for those who struggle to make friends or interact with others. It is essential to understand what is meant by special needs in order to help young learners develop positive relationships with their peers and improve their overall well-being and academic success.

After reading "The Blueberry Story," record your thoughts and feelings.

You may already know the Individuals with Disabilities Education Act (IDEA) is a law that provides guidelines for how schools in the United States should provide services and support to students with disabilities. However, if you do not, IDEA ensures special needs students have access to a free public education, where their needs are met, regardless of their disability, in the least restrictive environment. IDEA also requires schools to create an IEP for each eligible student with a disability, outlining their educational goals, accommodations, and services. Parents are given the right to participate in the decision-making process for their children and are granted protection rights for both the students and their families (U.S. Department of Education, n.d.). On the other hand, 504 plans, which fall under the Rehabilitation Act of 1973, ensure that individuals with disabilities are protected from discrimination (U.S. Department of Education, 2022b). IEPs and 504s, along with any other legal documents, such as services for gifted students, are the most common ones we see in schools and certainly keep us on our toes. Please remember, they are never optional.

In an article published by the University of California, Berkeley, Rebecca Branstetter (2020), school psychologist, author, and speaker, coined a clever saying: "connection is protection." Before instruction or procedures, "we need to tend to social-emotional needs first" (Branstetter, 2020). She added, "when students (and indeed adults) feel safe, seen, and supported, they experience more positive emotions, which boosts cognitive resources for learning" (Branstetter, 2020). Now this is powerful thinking. She speaks about social-emotional learning (SEL), which is the "specific skills and competencies that students need in order to set goals, manage behavior, build relationships, and process and remember information" (Jones & Kahn, 2017, p. 5). An SEL approach in teaching is especially critical for special needs students because it promotes their self-reliance, fosters a stable and strong relationship with the teacher, and helps them to learn how to manage their emotions effectively (Banks, 2022).

Branstetter's (2020) first principle in teaching with SEL in mind is the prioritizing of relationship building over academic rigor. I find it to be an exceptional mindset. I have pulled myself back many times when a student was not making progress and reflected on what I needed to do to strengthen the relationship. The second principle discussed is to be innovative when it comes to providing accommodation and support. Breaking down or chunking information, creating high-impact visuals, and modifying assignments to match what is most important to eliminate volume—quality over quantity and brain breaks for a needed reset in focus—can make a difference in student motivation and engagement. Finally, a collective effort among all staff and parents or guardians is crucial in ensuring students are immersed in a committed and nurturing atmosphere of encouragement. With you in charge of organizing and communicating with all educational constituents, students have the best opportunity for a bountiful education.

It can be overwhelming to keep all accommodations straight since each student is unique and their educational road maps vary. It takes a team. I experienced great value in reaching out to the administration, counselors, and special education staff for assistance in identifying students with possible needs and with sticking to the specifications in student legal documents such as IEPs. Learning from our colleagues can be instrumental in mentoring us as we recognize and tackle social, emotional, and academic needs, thereby fostering a positive and inclusive learning environment for all.

In this chapter, we will hear directly from experienced special education teachers to learn how they have supported students' unique needs, grasp how to navigate obstacles in the classroom with consistently applied positive measures, and know how to apply standard special education procedures organically to your classroom culture for the purpose of building bonds.

Understand Standard Procedures

There is a lot to know about educational legalese. I recommend developing a strong relationship with the special education staff through cooperative collaboration. This involves actively sharing ideas, knowledge, resources, and responsibilities through communication, trust, and mutual respect, all while keeping the student as the center focus. Following and understanding all specially designed instructions in IEPs, accommodations on 504 plans, and other official documents are also necessary. Some readers may already understand my urgency in explaining special needs requirements. However, for those who are uncertain, please allow me to become a tad clinical here for your benefit.

Visualize yourself at the beginning of the year as you are given access to multiple IEPs, 504 plans, GIEPs, and other legal documents for the students on your roster. With 7.5 million (2021–2022) students nationwide, from nursery school to college graduation, receiving special education services, it is likely you will have some documents to review and be required to know by heart (U.S. Department of Education, 2022b). Each year, I had at least fifteen to twenty to start. It took a lot of time and a careful eye to sift through them all and to know the legal requirements for each student by the time they arrived on the first day. These documents are of the utmost importance as they provide a framework for ensuring students receive support. "Effective IEP goals are strengths-based and SMART: specific, measurable, attainable, results-oriented, and time-bound" and assist students in achieving their full potential (The Understood Team, n.d.). An IEP reading goal example might be, "When given a grade-level text, student will read and demonstrate comprehension of grade-appropriate literary texts (e.g., stories, legends, poems)" (Lightner, n.d.). From this goal, you or the learning support teacher would create a plan to teach specific skills and monitor the progress of the student for, hopefully, goal attainment. In addition, specially designed instruction, or SDI, which defines adaptations, modifications, and instructional strategies tailored to meet student needs, would also be added.

Another very important document is the 504. The Rehabilitation Act of 1973 (Section 504) states:

> No qualified individual with a disability shall, by reason of such disability, be excluded from participation in or be denied the benefits of the services, programs, or activities of a public entity, or be subjected to discrimination by any such entity. (U.S. Department of Education, 2022a)

This may sound similar to an IEP. However, students with a 504 do not have goals and objectives like an IEP. A 504 plan provides accommodations for students who do not qualify for special education, but who may have a physical or mental disability. An ADHD (attention deficit hyperactivity disorder) diagnosis is an example of a disability that may need accommodation. It can be developed by a school team and may or may not include input from the parents or students. In my school, the counselor took care of spearheading the 504 documents. Some 504 examples include allowing extra time on tests and quizzes, providing notes, using nonverbal cues to refocus, alternative assessments, and special seating (Jones, 2022).

The IEP and 504 are common, but there are other documents for students who qualify for services, such as the GIEP (Gifted Individual Education Plan) and OHI. It is a big responsibility for educators to comprehend and adhere to these documents because they are vitally important—legally and ethically. Keeping organized can help. I have provided a quick reference table with accommodations you can adapt in figure 5.1 (page 76). It has

Student Accommodations	Jorge Doe (ES)	Jane Doe (ES)	Bryan Doe (ES)	Taisha Doe (ES)	William Doe (ES)	Carlos Doe (LS)	Nick Doe (I)	Peter Doe (LS)	Evan Doe (LS)	Kennett Doe (LS)	Jack Doe (LS)	Abigail Doe (LS)	Pat Doe (LS)	Rahul Doe (LS)	Silvia Doe (LS)	Kevin Doe (LS)	Kyle Doe (LS)	Mike Doe (I)	Aianer Doe (I)	Beau Doe (I)	Barbara Doe (I)
Extended Time on Tests and Quizzes		X				X													X		
Preferential Seating					X		X	X									X				X
Verbal and Visual Cues										X	X					X					
Chunk Large Tasks Into Smaller Ones				X		X				X			X			X		X			
Graphing Organizers and Sentence Starters										X	X					X		X			
Study Guides				X				X		X	X					X	X	X			
Check In and Check Out		X		X				X		X	X					X		X	X		X
Computer for More Than Two Paragraphs	X																				
Provide Wait Time							X			X			X		X		X				X
Adapted Tests						X	X	X		X	X									X	
Prompting to Ensure Focus	X										X			X							X
Frequent Checks for Understanding				X						X											
Repetition and Review of Leaned Material											X										
Restate Directions											X										
Guided Notes in Science and Social Studies			X			X				X			X					X	X		
Tests Read Aloud When Not Assessing Reading								X													
Work Area with Little Distractions		X			X									X				X		X	

Figure 5.1: Student accommodations.

helped me organize and implement requirements for my students with special needs. A good idea is to prepare the chart prior to the school opening. That way you will be ready since technically the services begin on day one! Providing the necessary ingredients for student success not only keeps you compliant with federal laws but also shows students you care and naturally strengthens your relationships with them.

Learn From Special Education Teachers

To gain a multifaceted understanding of *our* blueberries, I sought the expertise of some of the most exceptional teachers I have encountered who specialize in educating students with special needs. For our purposes, I will refer to them as the *teacher panel.* It was easy for me to select them since I know and trust them and have witnessed them in action over the years. Through individual in-person meetings or phone interviews, I provided an informal platform for these teachers to share their experiences and insights on establishing positive connections with their students who require specific accommodations in the classroom. They represented a range of school functions, including academic, English language learners (ELL), gifted, life skills, guidance, and emotional support. I was in awe of their passion as they spoke about teaching and establishing teacher-student relationships. Their strategies and teaching methods are compiled to help you with all your students, both with and without identified special needs. Other people's vantage points are helpful because we all have such mixes of differences in every class. No students are the same; no classrooms are the same!

Manage the Beginning Days of School

The first question I asked a cohort of special education teachers related, fittingly, to the first day of school and establishing teacher-student relationships. Most said they *do not* get right down to the nitty-gritty with rules and procedures. Instead, they aim to help students feel more important than a letter grade, textbook, or lesson by showing the students they are *authentic* and that they are more than a teacher. Like each student, this teacher is also a human who makes mistakes. They start facilitating purposeful conversations by sharing who they are and their likes and dislikes. Some of you may be more comfortable than others about sharing your feelings with your students, but it is the best way to show you are sincere. Students with special needs already have challenges when they enter school. Knowing their teacher is open, honest, and an advocate for them is key to helping them start the year on a positive note.

Letting young learners know you are human helps create a judgment-free zone and a place for them to feel safe. Sharing some personal details and using humor, if it comes naturally, can help reveal who you are and put students at ease. Finally, finding out about each student's passions and interests can go a long way in nurturing teacher-student relationships. This background knowledge allows you, throughout the year, to have conversations with them without always mentioning what they are learning or dwelling on classroom tasks. The teacher panel also recommends using light-hearted chitchat. Try not to take yourself too seriously. Nobody ever said that learning cannot be fun and productive at the same time. Have fun while being balanced, engaging, organized, and flexible. Open up with your students but, of course, remain the adult in the room.

Navigate Obstacles With Positivity

Maintaining teacher-student relationships, especially on bad days, can be a challenge. Maybe you have tried tactics such as ignoring a student's negative behavior or modeling positive behavior. You may have attempted to connect to their personal interests as a diversion tactic. Perhaps it was not enough. What do you do? When a student is having a difficult moment, day, or week, tapping into who *they* are can be calming for them and can create a unifying tone. First, make yourself available. Do a temperature check and ask how they are feeling on a scale from one to ten to gauge their moods and determine how you should intervene. An opportune time to do this is during the greeting time just before class starts. This gives you the advantage of defusing their day for them. Be discreet and let them know you are there to listen and your door is always open. Some students may only need a conversation to get back on track. Explain that you are noticing their atypical day. Show your awareness. Take the time to talk with students before problems escalate. Find out if they need some private time or a flash pass to the counselor to decompress.

This may come as a surprise, but it is OK to give yourself permission to lower the expectations for a student whose day spirals out of control. You are not giving in; you are just applying flexible adjustments to their routine or assignments. In the long run, you will get much further with them than pushing and demanding. Assure them that it is acceptable to take a different approach for that one day, such as completing fewer problems or reading a book instead of the assigned task. Make sure to emphasize that this is temporary, reinforcing that tomorrow they will be back on track like their peers. Acknowledging students lets them know they are noticed, and they crave to be seen. We all have bad days, and knowing someone is there is often enough to make things right. Another favorite tactic is allowing for choices. This can be a win-win situation because most students respond well when given options instead of commands, and at the same time, teachers are more apt to have better control. That said, while some choices can be beneficial, too many options can be debilitating. Depending on the student, be sure to strike a balance.

Overall, handling the student respectfully and assisting with personalized strategies are ways to differentiate. It shows that you recognize their difficulties without them losing their respect for you as a teacher. Even so, set boundaries so they do not abuse your willingness to help. You are not giving in and being their best friend. Instead, you are offering solutions and setting expectations as their mentor.

Finally, share a confidential heads-up with any other teachers a student may have and then follow up with the student periodically throughout the day. By demonstrating true interest in their well-being and understanding the reasons behind their off day, you demonstrate a strong sense of advocacy.

Sometimes, we run into obstacles even with positive measures in place. That is why strong communication with students' families is crucial from the beginning. Yet, parent or caregiver pushbacks do happen. Of course, parents want what is best for their children, and for the most part, they will be on board with your expertise. Moreover, numerous caring parents genuinely want what is best for their children and confidently trust us. Still, some feel their child is entitled to preferential treatment, even beyond their individualized plan. Others can be helicopter parents or the antithesis—not present. Dealing with difficult parents can be stressful and exhausting. Of course, you cannot control how parents feel, but you can control the atmosphere in your classroom. Also, if a parent challenges you, maintain a clear separation between any negative feelings you may have for the parent and your relationship with the student.

We already examined the importance of responding to parent emails immediately, even if it is just acknowledging receipt and letting them know when you intend to get back to them. For difficult situations, this can give you time to investigate their concerns and seek assistance from your administration if needed. If you feel miscommunication might occur via email, ask the parent when a good time is to call and the best phone number to reach them. Then, prepare. Write down what you want to say, cross off anything you feel would be antagonistic, reword it, and then call the parent back—or have them come to school for a more personal conversation. When you speak with them, present your perspective professionally and take your opinion out of the scenario. Acknowledge your intentions as different from what the child perceived. It is vital to keep the parent from being defensive. In the long run, applying practical and evenhanded steps under challenging situations will help you continue to bond with your students.

Create a Village

Enlisting the assistance of other professionals is essential in maintaining a solid relationship with any student. You may feel dejected that you are not every student's go-to teacher. Yet, some students need the proverbial village. It is helpful to involve other staff when they are available. Your administrator can be of great help. Create a list of ideas you have tried and ones you still want to try and share them. Ask if they can help you think outside the box. You do not want your meeting to sound like a venting session or like you are a complainer. They will respect the fact you came up with your own ideas and will hopefully offer some guidance and support. Invite administrators or other teachers to student presentations or activities, let students be helpers for others in the building, and create a lunch bunch composed of a cross-section of the student body and your students with learning differences. Solicit suggestions from your colleagues who are familiar with your students. They may be able to contribute to your idea collection—after all, we all have different lenses. Just ask. It is not a weakness. Ignorance is being a turtle and not exploring resources outside your comfy shell. Build a good rapport with all stakeholders, even the lunch personnel or custodians, as they might be useful in helping you with your students. I worked with our lunch staff in a bullying situation. Another set of adult eyes was crucial in that instance. Our custodian worked with me to keep one of my students organized. The student had extreme difficulty with this skill due to his ADHD, and our custodian checked in with him in the morning and throughout the day to keep him on track.

Navigate Conflicts and Achieve Harmony With Colleagues

Maintaining positive relationships with colleagues requires diplomacy. It is vitally important to be adaptable in certain situations and consider the cost-benefit analysis. Factors that can inhibit teacher-student relationships may include a colleague who disagrees with how you are dealing with your student. This is to be expected; after all, not everyone has the same approach. It is essential to respect colleagues' differences when they have the student's best interests at heart. An excellent way to handle this situation is to put the onus on yourself. Offer to help the colleague without blaming them. Use "I" statements and say something like, "This is what I saw, this is how the student felt, and this is what happened. How might I make sure it doesn't happen again? How can I help?" By sounding nonjudgmental, you will be less likely to put your colleague on the defense. Approach a tenuous situation as if you were dealing with a student by being respectful and tactful. You may need their support or valuable feedback to help your students. Cooperating and collaborating with your coworkers is an absolute plus in meeting your student relationship-building goals.

Understand the Role Counselors Play

The counselors in our schools play a pivotal role in the lives of students, especially those with special needs, known and unknown. Their expertise can be used by you in the classroom too. I had the pleasure of working with a counselor I think is the best in the world. She has the gift of helping students become the most independent people they can be. From the first day of school, she establishes herself as approachable and genuine. Using humor as her guide, she orchestrates connections to students' lives and her role as someone they can trust and depend on. She meets with each student individually to find out who they are, any problems they may have, and how they feel about themselves. She accomplishes this by reviewing their schedule with them, talking about their friends in the previous grade, and exploring their hobbies and interests. To record information, she prefers the old-school method of jotting down notes about each student on index cards that can be easily accessed when needed. She tries to make each student feel OK about themselves, creates a nonjudgmental space for them to meet, and is visible throughout the buildings. On the first day of school, she visits each classroom to greet students and begins to use their names immediately. Her job, she says, is to encourage them *not* to need her. She allows waiting time for them to solve their own problems but is always there as a safety net. She understands that giving students accolades for handling tasks and challenges themselves produces more independence. In turn, she helps students strike a balance in their lives. The takeaway: make sure you develop an open and cooperative relationship with your counselors because they can be beneficial in assisting you in connecting with your students.

Assess Experience and Evidence-Based Strategies

When you have students with special needs, try to think ahead. In my experience, I have found a heads-up approach to be a best practice. It is appreciated, especially by parents, because it can make the student feel empowered. Of course, when students are happy, most of the time the added benefit is parents feel the same. Provide behavioral and academic expectations, a brief explanation of the lesson with possible reading ahead of time, and any supplies they might need. In mathematics one idea is to review several concepts and problems or highlight key terminology before the lesson. Previewing by prereading text in other subject areas to ensure comprehension would also be helpful. Doing anything to make it easier for the student to feel prepared is an asset for them. As you teach, be conscious of time. Allow the student some wait time before answering. Using manipulatives to show, not just tell, adds dimensions and interest as you teach. Cueing is essential. Agree on a cue for keeping the student focused or for any needed assistance (Positive Action Staff, 2023). Break down tasks into attainable parts and note key dates as markers to complete larger projects. A stash of colored highlighters comes in handy to make your words (or dates) stand out and capture students' attention. Working in these ways is a big part of the relationship-building process because you are involving students in their education and letting them know they are valued.

Students with special needs often have difficulty with executive functioning, which is how our brains allow us to manage tasks, make decisions, and solve problems effectively. Basically, executive function is the "management system of the brain" (Belsky, n.d.). Some signs that indicate a student has difficulty with cognitive control are noticeable when a student has difficulty prioritizing or initializing tasks or creating a plan. Students who have poor time management, lack of flexibility, impulsive behaviors, focus and attention issues, or a poor working memory may struggle to retain information while completing assignments. The most difficult task for these students is often organization. One of our teacher panel participants noted that we need to simplify any complexities. This may include going through a student's assignment book and crossing off unnecessary dates, such as the weekends and days when school is not in session or writing in reminders for important upcoming dates and deadlines. Using task checklists and sticky notes for directions or positive notes can be helpful. Students need to be taught *how* to organize materials, books, and backpacks and create a system for filing papers. Colored-coded pocket folders for each subject seem to work best, but you may need management check-ins to make sure they stay organized. Seeing a student struggling with a mountain of papers and trying to find the right one for class is excruciating and breaks my heart. Just by taking a little time to help them organize, we can provide a better environment in which they can learn. Recordkeeping is essential for all our learners, especially students with special needs. Accommodations vary from student to student, and an organized method can assist with successful follow-through. Figure 5.1 (page 76) is an example you can use to see who needs what services more quickly. Please note: this document does not replace students' records such as IEPs and 504s. You are still responsible for knowing all student records.

Conclusion

Developing strong bonds with students is not an isolated concept. Students with challenging learning abilities need you to thoroughly know their accommodations or specially designed instruction and ensure the directives are followed. Doing so shows that you are an ardent advocate for them. You can be the champion for students when you see a need to change their educational plans or the hero who works alongside their other teachers, the special education teacher, instructional aides, parents, and administration to help them. And you can be known as the compassionate teacher who understands when their day goes south and they need a moment to regroup. Applying tools and strategies will make young learners *feel* and *be* successful. When you are *present* and *providing the necessities* for learning, you secure the foundation of relationship building. Some of the most fulfilling relationships with students I have encountered are with students who possess incomparable uniqueness. It may take extra steps to provide necessary services for them, but the satisfaction of seeing a student with challenges overcome obstacles can be one of the greatest gifts of our profession.

Typically, we see our students only while at school and are often blind to what transpires when they leave our doors. Remember, students are like blueberries; we never know what we will receive when the pallet unloads onto the dock. We cannot send them back. Instead, we must treat each student equitably, provide the unique resources they need for success, and hold them to high standards.

Besides students with academic challenges, we may teach some learners who struggle with their identity—whether it is gender, race, ethnicity, religious affiliation, cultural heritage, socioeconomic status, sexual orientation, or life experiences. In the next chapter, we will address diversity, its impact on students, and ways to be supportive so students feel included.

6

Cultivate Diverse Connections

Diversity is being invited to the party; inclusion is being asked to dance.
—Vernā Myers

While striving to build teacher-student relationships, we cannot ignore the concepts of racism, sexism, homophobia, transphobia, anti-Semitism, and other marginalizing behaviors; how they can impede our efforts; and in the end, prevent students from succeeding to the best of their abilities. Faculty in-service days in my school district centered around diversity, racism, and discrimination (overt and covert) and included tools for understanding and avoiding micro- and macroaggressions. To clarify, *overt racism* encompasses various manifestations of discrimination such as racially biased speech, stereotyping, gaslighting, xenophobic attacks (hatred), and expressions of prejudice. Whereas *covert racism* is more difficult to recognize because its presence can be "conscious or unconscious" like with microaggressions (Ni, 2021). The act of attending well-meaning workshops was the equivalent of pocket-sized reiterations of state and district initiatives. Don't get me wrong. They were a great start. However, I believe teachers and staff need more consistent professional learning opportunities to fully comprehend not just racism, but the effects of inequality and oppression as well.

Support for Students From Marginalized Groups

There are students, some of whom you may know, who suffer quietly from pronounced discrimination. Alarmingly, the statistics speak on their behalf. Since 1999, and every two years since, the Gay, Lesbian, and Straight Education Network, or GLSEN, has published the *National School Climate Survey* to provide data on the adversarial atmosphere of LGBTQ+ students (Kosciw, Clark, & Menard, 2022). In its 2021 publication representing all fifty states, 81.8 percent of LGBTQ+ students "reported feeling unsafe in school because of at least one of their actual or perceived personal characteristics" (Kosciw et al., 2022, p. xv). Upward of 80 percent of LGBTQ+ students heard homophobic, gay, or transgender negative remarks at school with 76.1 percent having suffered personal "verbal harassment" and 31.2 percent actually "pushed or shoved" (Kosciw et al., 2022, xvi). The United Nations Educational, Scientific and Cultural Organization (UNESCO) published in its *Global Education Monitoring Report 2020* that schools "fall far short of making students from all socio-economic backgrounds equally feel like they belong" (p. 81). The data do not lie. Educators must be the sturdy guide and anchor for students in need. Long-standing divisions need to be addressed directly and in thoughtful and informed ways to build relationships with students and help them thrive.

So, what is being done to address LGBTQ+ acceptance, especially in our schools? The Equal Access Act of 1984 was signed into law to allow for a safe and supportive environment for the LGBTQ+ community. Secondary schools across the nation offer an after-school hours student group called GSA, which stands for Gay-Straight Alliances or Genders and Sexualities Alliance. The group's purpose is to provide a positive, safe, and supportive school environment with a major focus on eliminating bullying and nurturing student allies (U.S. Department of Education, 2023).

A plethora of helpful information is available for educators online and in print. The following resources include selections to consider in your journey to educate yourself more thoroughly about those facing systemic injustice. Gaining a deeper understanding of LGBTQ+ students will assist you in making viable connections with them.

Online:

- www.stopbullying.gov
- www.cdc.gov/lgbthealth/youth-resources.htm

- www.hhs.gov/ocr/lgbtqi
- www.nea.org/resources-library/nea-lgbtq-resources
- www.thesafezoneproject.com/resources
- www.childwelfare.gov/topics/systemwide/diverse-populations/lgbtq/lgbt-families/
- www.thetrevorproject.org/public-education

Texts:

- *Gender, Bullying, and Harassment: Strategies to End Sexism and Homophobia in Schools* by Elizabeth J. Meyer (2009)
- *Reading the Rainbow: LGBTQ-Inclusive Literacy Instruction in the Elementary Classroom* by Caitlin L. Ryan and Jill M. Hermann-Wilmarth (2018)
- *The Gay Revolution: The Story of the Struggle* by Lillian Faderman (2015)
- *Little Learners, Big Hearts: A Teacher's Guide to Nurturing Empathy and Equity in Early Childhood* by Christine Mason, Randy Ross, Orinthia Harris, and Jillayne Flanders (2024)
- *LGBTQ Youth and Education: Policies and Practices* by Cris Mayo (2022)

Unraveling Racism

As educators, we must recognize racism as the proverbial elephant in the room that needs to be acknowledged and pursued, studied, and discoursed. Our students' relationships with us depend on our acknowledgment that racism is glaringly real; it is pervasive in our homes, community, school, country, and the world. Consequently, our willingness to listen and learn more about racism is unquestionably on our doorstep.

The United States has taken on the study of systemic injustice with an approach that examines the law and suggests that race is *not* biological in nature, but a socially constructed concept used to dominate and mistreat people of color. Furthermore, it is embedded in the legal systems and institutions of the United States (systemic racism) perpetuating social, economic, and political disparities between White and non-White individuals. Laws brought about by this new critical thinking have been passed in states nationwide impacting decisions by educators, like how and what to teach, the selection of educational materials, and lesson planning. States with enacted laws have mandated regulations from the banning of specific terminology and educational materials to imposing rules of *do this, not that.* This causes uncertainty and teachers in some states are confused and worried about overstepping boundaries or worse, losing their licensure (Belsha, Barnum, & Aldrich, 2021).

How did this topic become an educational initiative and why is there no commonality among the states? Gloria Ladson-Billings, professor emerita at the University of Wisconsin at Madison, has been researching social justice for decades and can provide some answers. She states, "Critical race theory is a theoretical tool that began in legal studies, in law schools, in an attempt to explain racial inequity" (as cited in Anderson, 2022). Beginning in the 1950s, society changed. We had the emergence of the Civil Rights Act, the Voting Rights Act, and eventually Affirmative Action. There was a shift in thinking with how we explained racial inequity. According to Ladson-Billings (as cited in Anderson, 2022), we moved from a genetics approach that was "baked into the way we have organized the society"; she believes social justice is "misunderstood" because other groups and concepts have been tossed under the topic umbrella, like the LGBTQ+ community and SEL. When she first started working with social justice, it was to detail racial inequities in education. It has become a political tool, causing divisiveness, which has found its way into our school system. Taking away meaningful discourse, debate, and core values does not benefit our students and can jeopardize the connections we build with them.

As professional educators, what can we do? How do we become more aware of racism, advocate for social justice, and serve our students? A good start is to make sure we understand the concept of racism in general and then consider how its impact on our students affects our objectives in building relationships with them. To start this thinking, consider the following standard definitions and then jot down your thoughts.

From *Merriam-Webster* (Racism, n.d.b):

> 1: a belief that race is a fundamental determinant of human traits and capacities and that racial differences produce an inherent superiority of a particular race
>
> *also*: behavior or attitudes that reflect and foster this belief: racial discrimination or prejudice

2 a: the systemic oppression of a racial group to the social, economic, and political advantage of another

b: a political or social system founded on racism and designed to execute its principles

From *Dictionary.com* (Racism, n.d.a):

1. a belief or doctrine that inherent differences among the various human racial groups determine cultural or individual achievement, usually involving the idea that one's race is superior and has the right to dominate others or that a particular racial group is inferior to the others.

2. a policy, system of government, etc., that is associated with or originated in such a doctrine, and that favors members of the dominant racial or ethnic group, or has a neutral effect on their life experiences, while discriminating against or harming members of other groups, ultimately serving to preserve the social status, economic advantage, or political power of the dominant group.

3. an individual action or behavior based upon or fostering such a doctrine; racial discrimination.

4. racial or ethnic prejudice or intolerance.

Using the preceding definitions to guide you, write your understanding of *racism*.

____

____

____

____

____

____

____

____

____

Evolution of Racism

Some of the words you may have chosen to describe racism may be power, domination, superiority, and marginalization. They conjure up dark historical periods, but they also seem to sustain through time. There are strong indications that racism still plays a significant role in perpetuating inequalities. In 2004, researchers conducted a study with White and Black American job applicants. Both groups were equally qualified and given much the same preparation as far as interviewing and dressing appropriately. Those who were Black had 50 percent fewer callbacks and job offers than their White counterparts. Moreover, between 1968 and 2016, the income disparity between White and Black families remained relatively unchanged, while wealth comparisons show an increased gap (Brooks, 2021). Rather than moving past racism, it is evident that it has continued to persist and permeate various aspects of society over time. There is a disconnect in the interpretation of how racism and the words we use to describe it affect people *in our current times.*

Occasionally, I have heard a student say, "that's racist," or "you're a racist," to another student. In most cases, the context was askew, and a misunderstanding of the true meaning of racism was lacking. I have heard some colleagues and friends claim they are not racist because they accept people of all colors and ethnicities, that all people are the same, and that they don't see differences. Renowned author Ibram X. Kendi (2019) begs to differ. When someone says they are not racist, it is a "claim that signifies neutrality" (Kendi, 2019). In this way, racism is neither perpetuated nor disavowed (Kendi, 2019). Essentially, when we say we are not racist, we take the easy way out and assume passivity. We cannot claim we are *Switzerland* (a neutral country) and hope to change our mindset. We need to be proactive.

Indeed, per Kendi (2019), to say we are "not racist" indicates we are neutral and do not acknowledge our dissimilarities. Claiming you are not a racist person does not signify your intentions to do something about racism. In a way, it suggests you are in limbo. Kendi (2019), instead, says we need to claim we are "antiracists." This term makes it clear we are not complacent, but we attest to racism's existence and are willing to help change a divided world. This also recognizes and celebrates the unique and special differences among all people.

We need to accept our differences and cultural specificities in our efforts to remove barriers in relationship building. Our plurality—our skin color, religion, customs, traditions, sexual orientation, social groups, experiences, and language—embodies us. Ask yourself: Is a tourist asking for directions in an unknown language, a neighbor displaying a Buddha statue in the backyard, or a family sitting down to dinner on the floor eating from one large dish without utensils similar to what you might find in your culture? We all look, act, eat, drink, and express ourselves differently. Therefore, to say we are not racist indicates we are neutral and do not acknowledge our dissimilarities, as Kendi (2019) has pointed out. First, we need to accept each other's differences and cultural specificities, celebrate them, and move forward to create a more balanced, vibrant society.

How do we address race in the classroom to preserve and nurture healthy teacher-student relationships? The answer is not simple but educating oneself through meaningful discourse with other professional educators, listening to podcasts and ebooks, and researching about race, are excellent places to start. The more you learn and examine all perspectives, the easier it will be to be open to the students in your tutelage. Never underestimate your power as a teacher. Your students look up to you.

Thoughts on Microaggressions

There is no doubt about it. Our students are diverse. They may be introverted, extroverted, Black, White, poor, rich, tall, short, neglected, loved, or abused. Like the blueberry story from chapter 5 (page 69), we take them all. Our students come to us with innumerable backgrounds and experiences, and we must be aware of and respect them.

As students interact with their peers, we must be vigilant observers and listeners. We aim to create an inclusive classroom where all feel valued and respected to help us build relationships with each student. However, even when using our eyes and ears to the best of our ability, microaggressions can sneak into the room. They can temporarily disrupt an equitable classroom learning environment and may leave scars on vulnerable young people.

Merriam-Webster defines a *microaggression* (n.d.) as "a comment or action that subtly and often unconsciously or unintentionally expresses a prejudiced attitude toward a member of a marginalized group (such as a racial minority)." When you facilitate discussions with your students on any subject, you should be aware of any microaggressions that may arise—from you or the students themselves. This is when your keen observations come into play. Be alert and listen intently, avoiding distractions because you do not want to miss anything.

To better identify microaggressions, let's examine some examples. Read each statement and check any that you feel are a microaggression.

- ☐ A student in your class has a long last name with letters that are difficult for you to pronounce. You decide to use your version of their name because it is easier.
- ☐ Your students' identifications of gender are varied, but you continue to refer to them as he or she.
- ☐ You speak loudly or with pronounced emphasis to a student in a wheelchair.
- ☐ You ask a student in class who has a slight accent, "Where are you from?"
- ☐ A student shares a connected but implausible personal experience with the class, and you do not respond. Instead, you call on the next student who has their hand up.
- ☐ You ask a student multiple times to repeat their response and tell them they speak too softly.
- ☐ Some heavy boxes need to go to the office, and you need volunteers. You call Jimmy, Mark, Bruce, and Marcus to help you.
- ☐ Your testing day falls on Rosh Hashanah, and you tell the class if anyone is Jewish, they can take it another time.
- ☐ A student asks another student for help in mathematics for no other reason than he is of Asian descent. The rest of the class laughs. You say nothing, divert attention, and move on with the lesson.
- ☐ You advise a tall student that the basketball team needs more players.

If you chose each example as a possible legitimate microaggression, you are correct! Some examples may seem inconsequential or may appear to rest on the fine line between being a microaggression or not. However, we cannot take microaggressions lightly. From a student's perspective, microaggressions can be humiliating and malicious. Not only that, but they are "corrosive" and can cause a downward spiral to the point of experiencing an attack on what I call the list of self-values: self-worth, self-acceptance, self-confidence, self-respect, self-image (positive), self-compassion, and self-care (University of Edinburgh, 2022). Lacking self-value can result in trust issues, strained relationships, failure to thrive, and poor attendance and interest in school. When all is said and done, microaggressions can make one feel inconsequential—completely insignificant—where feelings are difficult to counterbalance (University of Edinburgh, 2022).

Microaggression Examples

Here are some examples of microaggressions that, with time, have been remedied. Over the years, many of us in the profession have made a change instructing students to sit "pretzel style" or "crisscross applesauce" when joining on the carpet instead of "Indian style," which has historical roots as an ignorant and outdated term to refer to Native Americans. I have heard some educators use the phrase "Jew down," an anti-Semitic trope with connections dating back to medieval times. A standard description of this is called racial anti-Semitism. Furthermore, saying you have been "gypped" is a derogatory saying associated with Roma culture (Oster, 2019). What if one of these terms were accidentally used during a lesson or private conversation? It could offend students, cause damage to the teacher-student relationship, and, most importantly, stay with students in negative ways throughout their formative years. These terms can also be cumulative in their effect, impacting a young person's image of themselves and their place in the world over time. Moreover, even if not directed toward a particular student or culture, the acceptability of such terms is unfortunately modeled for students. Therefore, it is vital to avoid any kind of microaggressions directed at someone in the classroom. If you have unknowingly used insulting language or realized you said something that could be considered a microaggression, it is not the end of the world. Think of it as an opportunity for discussion. Express how you could have said what you said differently, and apologize. Contact the parents or guardians if necessary and consider a follow-up with the student after your discussion to make sure they still feel all right about the outcome. Mistakes are human, and acknowledging your misstep shows integrity and humaneness.

Another aspect to consider is that meanings may change over time and may have different connotations for individuals and groups. A term or phrase we have known for many years may seem ordinary to us but can be offensive to groups, cultures, or even individuals. In terms of school, there is no doubt about it: microaggressions can leave a student feeling disregarded, confused, and angry, and can trigger responses that may be invisible or behaviors that may not have been witnessed previously (Berk, 2017). Identifying and snuffing out microaggressions must be intentional so we do not project haphazardly while teaching. Moreover, if we as educators witness microaggressions and do not address them, we can be seen as apathetic and inequitable and, again, model an unacceptable response. Instead, a solution is to immediately take the time to address the situation privately if warranted and publicly if it will not offend or embarrass. The class will look for your reaction and judge how you handle the situation. Preparing in advance is prudent. Being mindful is a good start; also, be sure to attend sensitivity awareness training in your district or through coursework and collaborate with your colleagues to promote inclusivity in your school.

Unconscious Attitudes and Implicit Bias

Unconscious attitudes or stereotypes, or implicit biases, are "unconscious forms of discrimination and stereotyping based on race, gender, sexuality, ethnicity, ability, [and] age" (Tslpursky, 2020). For example, asking students where they are from due to their accent or appearance may seem like a friendly question. However, it can send a message to someone that they stand out from the crowd and are thus outsiders. Mistakes such as this can ostracize students unintentionally. Prior experience may have taught you that if someone has a different accent, appearance, or custom, they may not be from the United States. This information, stored in your unconscious mind, can spring forward almost involuntarily. Your childhood, education, and exposure to movies, books, media, and friendships have contributed to your unconscious or implicit bias. As an educator, you bring your background and experience with you into the classroom, so it is no wonder that biases can happen without recognition. In the Harvard EdCast *Unconscious Bias in Schools*, principal Tracey A. Benson observed a classroom where none of the four Black students participated (as cited in Benson & Fiarman, 2019). The way the teacher stood to teach prevented her from seeing them because the projector was blocking, and her back was toward them. After a period, she changed her position when teaching and began calling on the Black students. They became more actively involved as a result. Regardless of race, most teachers genuinely care for students and want what is best for them (Anderson, 2019). Now is a good time to take a deep breath. Unconscious biases do not arise from personal shortcomings. There is no need for shame or blame. Instead, it is more advantageous to use our energy to acknowledge biases' existence and keep a more vigilant eye on our behaviors (Tslpursky, 2020). Spark conversation with others about your biases and with any groups that might be affected, such as racial and ethnic minorities, women, LGBTQ+, individuals with disabilities, older adults, religious or cultural minorities, immigrants, socio-economically disadvantaged, or those with mental health conditions (Anderson, 2019). Another suggestion is to attend professional development opportunities. If you do not have access to any, go online to organizations like the Institute for Humane Education, where there are numerous links to training resources (Rakestraw, 2017). With serious soul-searching, awareness, and knowledge, you can shrink those sneaky unconscious biases in your life. It is not just a win for you, but a double bonus for you and your students as you build strong connections. Make your classroom a place where everyone feels like they stumbled on a treasure trove of understanding.

Sensitive Conversations About Oppression

Orchestrating more sensitive talks will create a vibrant learning environment, but how does a discussion begin, or how do you encourage discourse? A suggestion is to implement a learning environment that cultivates both creative thinking and exploration. In *Pedagogy of the Oppressed*, Paulo Freire (1968/2000) discusses educational "banking" or the concept of students "depositing" and "storing" information (pp. 71–72). In this way, teachers act as the authority or oppressor and students as the ignorant or oppressed. To put it precisely, the *I am* statement is the teacher in charge of educating the student with the knowledge that only they have, and the *you are* statement is for the student who receives the information. However, what is missing is the *we are* statement indicating that the teacher educates the student and vice versa. The latter shows, as Freire (1968/2000) says, "both are simultaneously teachers *and* students" (p. 72). Promoting higher-level thinking helps build teacher-student relationships because it enables dialogue and creates a safe space for exploration. Through problem-based learning and inquiry processes, educational barrier walls crumble; old-school instructional models are no longer used to bank learning, dismissing student apathy. This new freedom allows the oppressors (teachers) to be the guide on the side and not the sage on the stage. The oppressed (students) become lifted out of their world of ignorance into power over their educational and social circumstances. Freire (1968/2000) also believes:

> Students, as they are increasingly posed with problems relating to themselves in the world and with the world, will feel increasingly challenged and obliged to respond to that challenge. . . . Their response to the challenge evokes new challenges, followed by new understandings; and gradually the students come to regard themselves as committed. (p. 81)

Nonbanking pedagogy allows students to learn critically with profound free thinking, and it leads to supporting antiracism. Through conversation and learning that are focused more on inquiry, students will have the opportunity to connect with their own experiences and the world through the learning process. In turn, with students and teachers recognizing what makes us all unique, denial of our differences becomes invalid. An embrace of what makes us each special contributes to more balanced relationships with one another. Also, nonbanking pedagogy is a clear advantage to closing the achievement gap, a legitimate concern.

Please take a moment to read the following excerpt from *Pedagogy of the Oppressed* and reflect on it in the space provided:

> Banking education maintains and even stimulates the contradiction through the following attitudes and practices, which mirror oppressive society as a whole:
> (a) the teacher teaches, and the students are taught;
> (b) the teacher knows everything, and the students know nothing;
> (c) the teacher thinks, and the students are thought about;
> (d) the teacher talks, and the students listen—meekly;
> (e) the teacher disciplines and the students are disciplined;
> (f) the teacher chooses and enforces his choice, and the students comply;
> (g) the teacher acts and the students have the illusion of acting through the action of the teacher;
> (h) the teacher chooses the program content, and the students (who were not consulted) adapt to it;
> (i) the teacher confuses the authority of knowledge with their own professional authority, which they set in opposition to the freedom of the students;
> (j) the teacher is the Subject of the learning process, while the students are mere objects. (Freire, 1968/2000, p. 73)

Reflect on and rewrite any banking principles to promote better student creative thinking and limit learning passivity.

It may seem counterintuitive, but feeling *uncomfortable* can lead to *becoming* comfortable when talking about racism, biases, injustices, varying perspectives, and the like. At the building level in my district, I participated in professional learning and courageous conversations that made many of us uneasy. Choosing to ignore sensitive topics such as social injustices and all they encompass is not the best course if we hope to establish meaningful relationships with our students (Singleton, 2022).

Creating a welcoming and nonjudgmental learning environment helps all stakeholders feel more comfortable with sensitive discussions. As discussed previously, I have shared tidbits of my life with my students without giving up a level of privacy. For example, I talked about my children, pets, and hobbies. Being open to students about my personal life allowed many of my students to share their feelings, passions, and concerns. I realize that not every teacher has the capacity to step outside a reserved comfort zone immediately. If that is you, it will take time and practice. Interacting with less serious subjects at first can help pave the way to discuss delicate and critical topics such as racism as they occur.

Philadelphia educator Matthew R. Kay (2018) offers guidance on how to go about this in his book, *Not Light, But Fire*. He speaks with his students about wisdom, facilitates meaningful race conversations that can apply to other marginalized groups, and is an excellent relationship builder. Kay (2018) suggests remembering to check yourself and analyzing why you are nervous. He advises that it is critical to understand why you feel the way you do about addressing specific topics. With consistency, let students know you are continuing to learn, and when you make mistakes, admit them. To create an open and safe classroom environment, he advises being "humble" with your students—"reflect with and after with the kids" and be sure to create a "culture of listening" (Kay, 2018, pp. 16–17). It is challenging to find time to instruct and practice extra activities given our standards based–driven, all-consuming days. However, even a bit of time is a plus, and if time runs out, make sure you pick up the conversation later with "dangling" questions or comments taking precedence.

Ideally, we strive to create a school environment where every student feels a sense of belonging, regardless of their background. In Resmaa Menakem's (2017) book, *My Grandmother's Hands*, which focuses on intergenerational trauma, he emphasizes that we do not take away anything from anyone when we implement opportunities for *all* to experience a more inclusive environment.

Your classroom learning community must be equitable and enduring (Kay, 2018). It should also be a safe place for all. Think about how you can create a more inclusive culture as you research and learn for the benefit of all your students.

Thoughts on Educating Ourselves

How do we nurture healthy teacher-student relationships in a society of social injustices? How do we create a campus culture of acceptance and sensitivity? The answers are not simple, but necessity requires us to become more educated and more sensitive. As professionals, we cannot rely solely on structured coursework, one-shot workshops, or professional development ad hoc practices to feed our souls and move the needle toward being more informed. We can begin by being proactive ourselves by, for example, fostering meaningful dialogue with other educators, listening to podcasts and ebooks, and researching topical articles. Websites like https://learningforjustice.org offer excellent knowledge to broaden your perspective. On the site, you can find resources for promoting social justice and antibias education through articles, lesson plans, webinars, podcasts, and teaching strategies. Materials cover topics such as racial justice, LGBTQ+ rights, cultural diversity, and inclusive classrooms. Adding rich and noteworthy books about racism to your knowledge base helps build understanding and develop multicultural competency. For example, the graphic novel *Stamped From the Beginning* by Kendi (2023) and illustrated by Joel Christian Gill takes a candid look at antiracism from various historical perspectives. Another option would be to read some of the books included in the references. These are written by some of the most powerful and passionate people of our time and their words are begging to be read. I recommend Kay's (2018) *Not Light, But Fire.* Kay is a teacher in Philadelphia who wrote from his own experiences. He speaks with wisdom and focuses on facilitating better conversations, and how you can be an excellent relationship builder.

Without consistent goals addressing inequity in our schools, our role remains static. So does our relationship with students. We cannot afford to remain in our heads just because it is comfortable, and it is what we have always done. Through self-exploration and education, the opportunity to build confidence and self-efficacy is waiting. The more you learn, the easier it will be to communicate with students and make stronger connections with them. Students are curious; they wonder how to deal with inequity.

Your students look up to you and take note of your words, attitudes, and actions. Never underestimate your power as an educator.

Conclusion

You may not agree with all the content of this chapter, but please keep an open mind. Ask questions. Collaborate with your colleagues, friends, family, neighbors, children, instructors, and administrators. Educate yourself. To move forward in education, and within society, there is an urgency to recognize and appreciate our differences. An example of a mission statement for developing outstanding teacher-student relationships in the classroom might be, *With students and teachers identifying what makes them all unique, denial of differences becomes invalid. An embrace of what makes us each special contributes to a more balanced relationship with one another.* These are powerful words to remember when educating young learners and perfect for displaying in the classroom as a reminder for all.

Consistent goals, courageous conversations, continuing education, and diversity training's impact on our students and society can positively affect our relationships with students. We cannot afford to stay in our own heads because it is what we have always done. Building positive relationships with our students—whatever background or differences—may include uncomfortable moments and extra time and energy, but they are worth it in the end. One of the most challenging jobs for us, but one of the most rewarding outcomes for our students, is to create a classroom where equity reigns. Perspectives on what is fair and balanced may differ for you and the students you teach. Yet, an open classroom environment with rich discussions and relationship building is necessary to avoid assumptions and judgmental behavior. This includes talks about sensitive issues too. It is a tall task by any stretch. However, we *all* miss things, even with the best intentions. That is OK. As long as we try, learn, keep moving forward, and create a safe space, we can inspire our students to develop and explore, and we can build meaningful relationships with them. In the meantime, they will develop healthy self-images, confidence, and respect for others, celebrate differences, and realize remarkable achievements. And that is a beautiful thing!

7

Create an Inclusive Environment by Responding to Student Voices

For all students to excel, teachers must learn about them and connect with each child. This is not just about finding out how they learn, but it is finding out who they are.
—George Couros

In addition to those students who experience racism and LGBTQ+ intolerance, others can feel plagued. Various factors can cause bullying, exclusion, and discrimination (such as appearance, abilities, emotional or academic challenges, and lack of social skills). We must ensure students are not overlooked in the teacher-student relationship-building process. The best rewards in education come from meeting *all* students where they are and guiding them to success through our meaningful relationships with them.

To be inclusive requires making each person feel welcome, valued, and respected. In the classroom, this means no exclusions or leaving anyone out. Did you ever have an instance where you did not feel part of a group? I recall being picked last for a basketball game in gym class. The teacher always allowed two student captains to choose their teams. After several agonizing moments, I was the last one picked. A cloud of insignificance enveloped me. Even today, I can visualize the entire scene. Our students can feel like they are not part of the team too—that they do not belong. These uncomfortable experiences and mindsets can linger into adulthood.

For this reason, we must be conscious coaches in the classroom, ensuring all students feel included. Inclusivity requires us to be watchful observers, seeking out students who might feel alone or disconnected. It is an enormous task, but it is the necessary foundation for building solid relationships. Otherwise, our intentions are simply and sadly half-baked. In this chapter, we will review specific student scenarios that characterize the variety of experiences students uniquely have in school and follow up with concrete general behavioral practices educators can implement to address culture and diversity, gender, student behavior, and parent-educator relationships.

Student Voices

A valuable way to understand these inequities is to see them from a student's perspective. The pages ahead offer short but factual accounts of student experiences at school. Some were obtained from my interviews with students, in which I asked, "What experiences will you remember from school when you are sixty?" Other accounts are from personal interactions with students over the years. As you read and hear their voices, think about how you could have been a bright light for them during the difficult times they describe.

Implicit Biases

A teacher pulled a Black female student aside in middle school and advised her to consider playing basketball in college. This encounter was odd to her. She will never know if it was due to her height or skin color. To this day, she frequently witnesses other microaggressions in school, along with bullying. She said the biggest obstacle in her school is so many other students, including friends and teachers, do not take racism seriously. If she could tell her teachers anything today, she would ask that they have more productive race conversations and better understand microaggressions.

We must first understand our implicit or unconscious biases to foster productive discourse. That means discovering any assumptions, stereotyping, or unconscious attitudes we may have. In this student's account, the teacher could have talked to the student about her future plans. Instead, he assumed that she was going to college and that she might want to play basketball there. Although he may have thought he was showing interest in her well-being, it backfired and certainly did not assist him in building their relationship. To unearth more about your implicit biases, it is necessary to take a deep dive to find out what they are. I suggest utilizing free online courses such as the University of North Carolina's comprehensive learning modules called Project READY: Reimagining Equity and Access for Diverse Youth (Project READY, n.d.). This is a resource for learning more about microaggressions, discussing race, or understanding what equity entails. By becoming more aware of microaggressions and learning more about them, you can proactively prevent future uncomfortable situations.

Assumptions About Religious Identity

Another student's ninth-grade social studies class studied world religions. To review before the test, the teacher divided the class into teams to play *Jeopardy!* When it came to the question of naming a Jewish holiday, her team turned to look at her, presumably because she is Jewish. She is introverted, which made her feel uncomfortable, and she responded with sarcasm and humor to deflect her discomfort. The teacher did not step in, nor would there have been time to do so in such a fast-paced game. It is challenging for introverted young learners who experience microaggressions.

Another teacher was proactive in his approach with her. This teacher realized she did not like to be called on in class and felt more comfortable and productive when not sitting in a group. Therefore, he assigned her a seat near his desk. He included her in discussions but asked questions requiring only a yes, no, or nod of the head as an answer. For example, he asked, "Isn't that right, (student name)?" as he taught a lesson. The teacher's actions—which took moments, not hours—significantly impacted this student.

Getting to know your students on a deeper level makes it easier to read their reactions and avoid situations where they may feel uncomfortable about their cultural identity. When you see possible instances where a student may feel marginalized, check in with them privately to ensure their feelings have not been hurt. Above all, be an ally, not a standby (in a state of inaction).

One of the best ways to ensure students do not feel like their identities are ignored is by creating a culturally responsive environment where there are role models and where they can "embrace their own culture and heritage" (Lynch, 2016). Developing an atmosphere of inclusivity leads to longevity in respect, acceptance, and the value of diversity within a school. It creates a sort of bandwagon effect by influencing the students, staff, parents, and community to be on board with inclusive practices (Bowman, 2020). A perfect example of growing cultural sensitivity is how our English language development teacher began an international festival, eventually merging with the world language department's multicultural fair. Students collaborated to create meaningful displays with colorful pictures, anecdotes, animated

animated stories, and tasty food samples from their cultures. When it came time to showcase their creations, classes cycled in to enjoy the exhibits and passionate work. How do I know it was successful? It grew to over one hundred participants. Trust me, it was one of the year's highlights, and we all enjoyed exploring and appreciating each other's cultures. In addition to other equity events and clubs, this festivity served to bind the cultures of our school together.

For educators, two excellent resources are the Anti-Defamation League (www.adl.org) and Simon Wiesenthal Center (www.wiesenthal.com) websites, which provide valuable resources for educators addressing cultural biases, stereotypes, and strategies. These sites offer excellent information about anti-Semitism, anti-hate, and antibias education programs and lesson plans, tools, and strategies for educators.

Microaggresions

As a self-proclaimed shy young man, a student recalls a time with an overly exuberant teacher. She always tried too hard to connect with him through his Jewish heritage. In front of the class one day, she played the national anthem of Israel and asked him to sing along. She had not asked him first. He declined, and she played the song on her phone instead. This teacher was pleasant, but he will remember this moment forever because she put him on the spot. Many of his friends' reactions were indifferent. However, he knows his feelings would have been more pronounced if he had been in a different class with peers he did not know.

We can try so hard to connect with students that it can cause them to feel singled out and uncomfortable. We must be careful that our efforts do not backfire and become microaggressions. This student believes individual personalities and group dynamics affect his feelings. In other words, the same scenario can feel different from one classroom to another, depending on the situation and who the players are. The student's level of comfort or discomfort and the reaction or nonreaction of others can determine the degree of microaggression perceived by the student; even so, that does not mean microaggressions are appropriate under any circumstances.

One student was in elementary school. As a sensitive child, she was saddened by what she heard the teacher say to one of her peers. Students had already learned about Diwali and were preparing to learn about Kwanzaa. The teacher walked over to a Black student and said to him in front of everyone, "(student name), do you celebrate Kwanzaa?" The student replied,

"What's Kwanzaa?" This response speaks to the ignorance in thinking we know everything about our students, and it should hasten our obligation to use discretion wisely.

The Derek Bok Center for Teaching and Learning (2003) at Harvard University has a tip sheet for teachers in multicultural classrooms needing inclusive teaching strategies. They propose two cardinal rules: "Learn as much about and become as sensitive as you can to racial, ethnic, and cultural groups other than your own," followed by the number two rule, "NEVER make assumptions about an individual based on the racial, ethnic, or cultural groups he or she belongs to. Treat each student first and foremost as an individual. Get to know students individually" (Derek Bok Center for Teaching and Learning, 2003, p. 2). This center poses thought-provoking questions and applicable ideas for exploring and developing a more inclusive classroom (Derek Bok Center for Teaching and Learning, 2003).

Sensitive Content and Offensive Language

One student's sixth-grade reading class was about to read a book about slavery. His teacher pulled him aside to tell him there would be offensive words in the novel. The teacher offered to meet with him if he needed to talk and debrief as they read. Then, the teacher advised the class about the language. As the reading progressed, the student could handle the narrative because he, and his peers, had been prewarned and sensitized. He recalled one student looking around the room for reactions, but the class was static.

The same student remembered a year earlier when he had just performed in a band concert and was walking back into class. Seemingly out of nowhere, another student called him an offensive racial term. He told the teacher, who then told the principal, who came to the room. The student who uttered the term said he had no idea what it really meant. The principal then asked the student victim if he believed the other student did not know the meaning. The answer: "No."

This account taught this student that having those in leadership capacities stand by you is comforting and provides a safe learning environment. Our student was unsure how the perpetrator was punished, but he was pleased the principal checked in with him regularly to ensure it did not happen again and made it clear his door was always open to talk.

Making Harsh Judgments

It was not this student's choice to enter school each day with her unkempt hair and clothing. Even so, she sometimes heard whispers from teachers about her appearance and home life. She was humiliated and felt their disgust.

Her background provided perspective. Due to her biological mother's drug abuse, as a baby, she was placed in foster care with a parent who had nine other foster children. In this house, abuse was the norm, and she often went to school with bruises. Some might blame the student and ask, "Why did she not let us know?" However, this student believed that not saying anything was better than facing possible dire consequences if she had told. She might go from a frightening home to no home at all.

In school, she cried often and acted out. The school observed her and filled out forms that convinced a doctor to prescribe subduing medication. Indeed, she was kept quieter, but she remembers being so tired that she fell asleep in class and, at one point, even drooled on herself. Her teacher once embarrassed her by ordering in front of others, "Go take your medicine." The symptoms she had were merely emotions of what she was going through. She felt the teachers, administration, and staff would never know the "real her" because the medication altered her thinking and behavior.

Time. It could have made a difference in this young person's life. It takes time to get to know a student, especially one dealing with extreme home issues. We do not know from where they come. We do not know what goes on behind even the most pristine-looking front doors. While medication can be helpful in many cases, it may not be the answer in some situations. She always wondered why her biological and foster mothers did not fight for her and why her teachers did not either. She thought if her teachers had invested more time with her instead of advocating for medicine, they would have gotten to know her authentically.

This student wants you to know that teachers make a difference, both positively and negatively. Sometimes, it just means taking a little extra time and expressing compassion. She had a first-grade teacher who saw a glimpse of what she was living. The teacher's words still resound even though the student is now a young adult: "I will *never* not love you." Sometimes, it does not take much to give love to students. Even if they cannot completely open up due to fear, they can still receive positive words of support.

What she was given, in a sense, she is paying forward today as she gives back to her community by helping others out of the depth of abuse, poverty, and seemingly impossible situations.

Making judgments is part of human nature—sometimes good, sometimes bad. Decisions are less troubling, though, when we focus on positive student characteristics. As educators, we can assist students more profoundly when we harness our emotional energy of empathy and compassion while accepting their cultural differences (Mental Health First Aid USA, 2019).

Ways to Prevent and Handle Bullying

One student came to school appearing disheveled and confused. His hair was in disarray, and his pants and shirt recalled their purchase from earlier years as they tried to keep up with his tall frame. As with many students on day one, he had difficulty with his locker combination, but he managed to pry it open after six assisted tries. Making it from class to class in his new middle school environment was challenging. However, he did not look frustrated. Instead, he seemed locked in his own world, perfectly content. As I learned more about him, he reminded me of an absent-minded professor—brilliant but socially unskilled. In the classroom setting, his peers shunned him at times, and it took some work on my part to create an environment where he was respected and not ignored. From what I understand, he did not have it so easy in other classes, in the hallways, or on the bus with other students harassing him. There are socially awkward students within most student populations, but in his case, he seemed unaware. Still, it is not wise to assume that he did not feel affected by marching to his own drum.

As we saw in the previous account, sometimes we have bits of information that can be helpful to know about our students who go through tough times. However, as in this current situation, I was blind. There was nothing to go on to establish a connection with this student. When this happens, reaching students is more difficult, and we may need more patience. I tried many strategies to make sure he felt included. I wanted him to become an integral part of the class. From experience, I feared he might be bullied since he appeared to dress and act so differently than the others. Preemptively, I invited him to be my tech person in case I had trouble, used humor, and tried to spark short conversations. I also involved the counselor, principal, and other teachers, having them casually speak with him at lunch or in the hallways. Additionally, I invited him to one of the clubs I sponsored and spoke with his parents, which should have been more helpful. It was not until I assigned him as the coordinator of a collaborative group project that he began to flourish. It was like magic. Seeing him in that capacity was rewarding and worth the effort!

Although I was unsuccessful in communicating with him on a personal level, I was able to tap into his brain intellectually. Eventually, he assumed other leadership roles and devoured challenging tasks. It was incredibly moving to watch how he became more communicative around the content we were learning and how other students grew in their respect for him.

In another student's experience, it was a new school year, and he was transferring to a public school located in a small, tight-knit community. From the beginning, he was teased and bullied because he was an outsider. One day, another student put him in a neck hold during class. The teacher pretended not to see. Unfortunately, what followed is unconscionable. The parent, not the principal, had to ask for a meeting to provide the details of the incident and ensure her son would be safe. During the meeting, the principal's response was cavalier as he explained that he had to go through hard times of this sort at his age. In other words, he conveyed that having a peer put you in a chokehold is something every young boy must go through, almost like a rite of passage. Let us be clear here. Dismissiveness has no place in school. Because the altercation was not correctly addressed, this young man will carry this trauma forever.

As mentioned in a prior chapter, we all come into the profession with varied education, experiences, and personalities. These are our core beliefs, and they affect how we respond to a bullying incident. Here is why. Our values are directly linked to empathy. Therefore, our level of empathy can determine the difference between intervening or ignoring a threatening situation between or among students. The more empathy we have, the more likelihood we will step in and handle a hostile situation. For the victim, your acknowledgment and action can show them they are valuable and worthy of fairness. In turn, the perpetrator learns that you are in charge and that they cannot get away with any harassment. Furthermore, teachers with more self-efficacy tend to have higher empathy toward others (Barni, Danioni, & Benevene, 2019). When you find confidence in knowing you can handle altercations, you are more likely to exhibit empathetic behavior, which, in turn, can assist in more positive situational outcomes.

Showing Compassion

This student was shy and sullen when we met. Although she paid attention in class, she rarely spoke. I noticed early on a pattern of incomplete homework. In speaking with her father, I found that her mother had breast cancer and was about to have surgery. This period began at a dark time in her life. She frequently missed school. When she was present, she often could not tolerate being around peers and visited the counselor instead. Knowing she needed a safe, quiet place to work, I suggested she use the small office nook across the hall from my room. Keeping the door open, I could keep an eye on her and teach the rest of the class. What I did not see was her life at home. Her father shared that her mom had a rough post-surgery.

Along with the anxiety associated with having a mother with a life-threatening illness, she had two younger siblings. Taking on the mother's role in the household, her efforts and late nights helping them left her exhausted. The room across the hall from me became a safe haven, enabling her to come to school and do her assignments. This student's terrible life event could have taken her life journey on an alternate course. Today, she is a vibrant, career-minded young woman. And the mom just celebrated eight years cancer-free.

I learned from this experience to always keep this simple but impactful personal mission statement in mind: *never give up on any student.* In our profession, we come across students who resist us, do not want to learn, have outbursts, and are sullen, disrespectful, or indifferent. You choose whether to make a positive or negative tattoo on their heart. Remember, they are coming to you *as is.* Try not to take it personally. For a student to be recalcitrant, something has happened to them outside of your control. You do not have to solve all their problems, but it is important to apply what you have learned and intuitively understand to create an environment where they feel socially, emotionally, and academically supported and secure.

In another student's eighth-grade year, I became his best friend. I know this because he told me. As flattering as that may sound, it is sad when I think about how most of his friends went on with their lives and his stood still.

The incident occurred during a social studies class. This student's friends tossed pretzels into each other's mouths to see how many they could snag. He thrust his head back for a catch and accidentally slammed his head into the concrete block wall behind him. He did not remember much after that. He could not even write his name legibly in the coming days. Unfortunately, this student sustained a traumatic brain injury that would take years to mend. I became his homeschool tutor. Each visit was extremely taxing for his brain, causing massive headaches. Gone was his social life, and even multimedia and social media had to be limited since they contributed to a rise in his headache pain scale. Most friends lessened their contact with him. I worked as a liaison between him and his teachers by securing and modifying the assignments. Most were supportive, but I sensed that a few questioned the authenticity of his injury. Yet, I could see the real student because I spent so much time with him.

Eventually, he finished the year but still had a long healing road ahead. I continued to tutor him periodically, and he progressed exponentially throughout high school and he reconnected with some of his friends. Today, he is a successful nurse at one of the best hospitals in his region.

This student needed a teacher and a friend. It was not unusual for his age-level friend contacts to dwindle. Unfortunately, there is no protocol for prolonged illnesses. When someone is initially sick, many of us provide notes, cards, and meals over time. When someone dies, there are cards, flowers, the funeral, and outreach to provide support. However, the in-between times seem to be lacking. In the middle, "We have no rituals for the grief that keeps on giving or the stress that becomes a way of life" (Hartwell-Walker, 2016). I quickly realized that my role as his tutor was not just about helping him catch up with his peers academically; it was equally important for me to provide ongoing friendship and support.

Early in my tutoring with him, he could not handle a bombardment of content or learning activities. Knowing this, I shifted gears and devoted about fifteen minutes to listening to his accomplishments since our last session and learning more about his interests. He needed this time to settle into any instruction. In time, this facilitated a friendship bond that helped him to learn and heal. A triangle of support formed: me, him, and his lovely family. Through this experience, I discovered that with impaired students, we need to put our relationships *first* and take their pulse for instructional direction and content pacing before jumping into the curriculum.

General Behavioral Practices for Educators

Some educators have a natural ability to create inclusive classrooms; others mean well but may struggle with finding ideas for how to do so intentionally and regularly. One way to start is to review the following list of suggestions, some based on the wisdom I have gained during my career. You may find a few ideas to weave into your repertoire. As you will see, some are general practices for relating to students; others relate more directly to diversity. However, all lead to inclusivity and, in the end, better teacher-student relationships.

- When students enter your room, treat them as kids first before addressing them as students. Use something current to spark a quick conversation among the group (Kay, 2018). It is often our nature to dive in immediately with the lesson. Allowing just a few minutes can create an incredible sense of community, worthiness, and comfort for the students.

- Reiterate that you are willing and open to helping your students. Knit that attitude into your lesson or at the end of each period or day. Change it up, though. Avoid using the exact wording every time.
- Turn off assumptions about behavior. Take the golden rule approach and treat each situation the way you would want if the tables were turned. For instance, if a student puts their head on the desk and often falls asleep, think about what would cause them to do that. Perhaps you would have done that if you pulled an all-nighter or had a disruptive sleep. Approaching the student from a noncombative perspective could mean a difference in your relationship with them. One time, I taught a student whose eyes closed on and off almost every day, even during the exciting parts of the lessons. I found that he fed, bathed, and cared for his infant brother and two other young siblings because his mother worked in the evenings. No wonder he was tired. I had another student who was very argumentative with me. It turned out his mother was verbally abusive. Sometimes, the factors that make our students act the way they do are out of our hands, but they can help us to understand them.
- Be honest. Students can see right through you. Do not think you can pull off being insincere or evasive. It is best to admit uncertainty and be humble. They will respect you for that, and you will add to your creation of a safe space.
- Let your students know you are approachable by ensuring they write down (or carry) copies of your contact information for email and district-approved social media.
- Go the extra mile. Think of ways to support your students outside of the typical instructional day. For example, let them know you popped into a baseball game or band concert.

Address Culture and Diversity Intentionally

Times have changed exponentially since the 1980s. Meeting diversity, equity, and inclusion (DEI) head-on is a must, and we are no longer in the age of complacency. Nonpartisan research has shown that:

> As the nation becomes even more racially diverse from the "bottom-up" of the age structure, more attention needs to be given to the needs and opportunities for America's highly diverse younger generations. The demography alone dictates that this will be necessary to ensure success for these youth and the nation as a whole. (Frey, 2020)

Take an audit of your cultural responsiveness. If you have already shifted your mindset to more inclusionary practices, bravo. However, I suggest baby steps and a no-pressure approach if you recognize a need for change. The following suggestions can point you in the right direction to develop a more conscious effort. Infusing your attitude and environment with more cultural competence shows you are moving toward an all-embracing direction. My final thought here is to remember to share what you have learned. Communicate with your teammates and other staff members. Sharing benefits everyone, including each student!

- Turn off assumptions about appearance and heritage. As the student mentioned earlier who was told she should play basketball in college, we must be mindful of how our words may marginalize our students. Just because a student looks like they may fit into a particular culture does not mean they ascribe to anything or everything within that culture. A student born in India may or may not celebrate Diwali or Christmas, speak Hindi, or follow the teachings of Buddha. Also, in our multicultural society, those at home may not share the same appearance or background as the student. This is another reason it is crucial to know your students individually. Never assume.
- Embrace all cultures and differences. Use the student resources you have at your disposal to facilitate a multicultural community where all learn from one another and flourish. Early in the school year, I always talk about my background. I talk about my family, pets, hobbies, teaching career, and also my ancestry. I mention that part of my family is Jewish because my brother married a Jewish woman and converted to her religion. I explain how I

have experienced some aspects of the Jewish faith through my niece's naming after birth and her bat mitzvah. Invariably, this creates a connection with some students of the Jewish faith and those familiar with Jewish cultural traditions such as a bar or bat mitzvah.

- If sanctioned by your school, recognize all religions and beliefs. Make a conscious effort to learn and discuss all ways of understanding the world. If you are addressing one religion, address them all, whether or not there are students in your class who hold those beliefs. Also, respect that some students may not come from religious backgrounds. Once you know your students, your list of beliefs to acknowledge will expand.
- Do not pigeonhole inclusion. For example, instead of siloing Black history into February, infuse your yearlong curriculum with notable authors, stories, and examples of Black achievement, no matter what subjects you teach.
- Plan ahead. Try to incorporate a representation of diversity through activities, authors, and lessons within each unit. It is easy and natural to infuse your curriculum with more diversity awareness. For example, if teaching about the moon from a science or history teacher's perspective, you could include the works of Katherine Jackson. She created the mathematical calculations for orbiting and landing on the moon. If you teach food science, you might incorporate an aspect of the 1990s cooking program *Iron Chef*, which originated on Japanese television, or your class might explore how bread is made differently worldwide.

Address Gender Appropriately

According to the U.S. Department of Education (2021), "Every student deserves to learn in a safe and supportive setting, free from discrimination. . . . Discrimination based on sex—including sexual orientation and gender identity—isn't just wrong, it's *prohibited* in America's schools." To support all our students, including LGBTQ+ students, consider some recommendations to give them a sense of safety at school. If you embrace any of these suggestions, you demonstrate a commitment to dismantling stereotypes and fostering a more inclusive student environment. Avoid using generic gender verbiage. Saying the phrase "boys and girls" is unnecessary, and it is passé given current gender understandings. Take students who identify as nonbinary. They do not identify as male *or* female and may feel they are being stereotyped (Black, 2020).

- One colleague I know used a brilliant replacement: the word friends. For example, say, "Friends, take out your project," or "It is time to pack up, friends." By referring to them in a familiar way such as this, do not worry that you will be giving up control. Students always know who is in charge in the classroom.
- Avoid gender grouping. Not all students may identify with the gender you may think they do. I know of a student who refused to work with anyone, boy or girl. I discovered that the student did not identify as a boy or girl and wished to be referred to as *they*. Being told to be in a specific boy or girl group was uncomfortable. As preferred, that student worked on a group project alone for most of the year. Gender grouping may imply that academic or behavioral expectations differ by gender.
- Advertise that your classroom is gender-neutral and accepting. Some examples are displaying a sign "All Genders Welcome," or hanging pictures of nontraditional activities for students (Prismic, 2019).

Abide by Respectful Classroom Norms

We have tremendous power over classroom standards. The environment we create is a microcosm of society where students learn and interact with one another. As educators, we can shape the learning environments, set expectations, and establish norms that promote inclusivity, respect, and equity. The look of our classroom, the verbal (unconscious or conscious biases) and physical (unconscious or conscious body movements) signals we share, and what we incorporate into our lessons give our students a giant heads-up about the kind of person we are and what they may expect to feel and learn. Do we honor respect in our classroom? Are our actions equitable among all? Do we provide flexibility when needed? Is our classroom atmosphere, pedagogy, and humanness conducive to learning? With introspection and thoughtful examination, you can begin by considering your teaching content. In each lesson, how can you integrate current events, add student cultural connections, or weave in the theme of diversity? Think about how your lesson may affect those in your class. Could anyone be offended or hurt by its content? Sift through the course material and weed out anything counterproductive to promoting inclusion (The President and

Fellows of Harvard College, 2024). Planning with these questions in mind is wise to ward off any possible uncomfortable moments.

- Acknowledge and address inappropriate behavior and language. Do not ignore the situation if a student uses words to intimidate another student. It is easier to go on with your day, but the message you send tells the victim they do not matter enough for you to intervene. And it also implies the offender can get away with being cruel. You risk not being respected by the other students as well.
- Avoid using generic *parent* verbiage. We must remember that some students may have no parents, one parent, could be fostered, raised by grandparents or other relatives, or may have two dads or two moms. Saying something as simple as, "Have your mom and dad sign the paper" or addressing a note to the "parents of ________" could be enough to upset a student. If the school holds events that include families, it is more appropriate to title an event, for example, a "special person" lunch instead of a "parent lunch." Even when it comes to homes, some students may be experiencing homelessness or living in a shelter.
- Create celebrations. Regularly set time aside for heralding the accomplishments of your students. Get them involved in the process to make it more meaningful for all. Your accolades are welcome and appreciated, but kudos from peers are even more powerful and uplifting.
- Respect privacy. Students who are timid and shrink from the spotlight still need TLC. Anticipate and honor their level of willingness to participate and remember that just because they are quiet does not mean they are *not* learning. These students may feel more comfortable speaking with an adult than with peers; if so, you might spark a conversation before or after class with them. In addition, you should not assume a student is eager to share an experience, cultural or otherwise, just because their life perspective might lend itself to the lesson.
- Know and remember student names. Write down difficult names phonetically and practice learning the correct pronunciation. A good tactic can be having each student speak their name into a recorder on the first day of school to not single out those whose

names are more difficult for you to pronounce. Then, you can review those privately. During this time of learning names, my students loved it when I gave out a small prize whenever I mispronounced a name. It kept me in check! Also, do not give students nicknames unless they have initiated one first.

- Provide appropriate learning spaces. Being inclusive requires allowing every student a working area to achieve their personal best. In my room, there were designated spaces students could use while completing individual or group work. Some students had mandated areas per their IEP or 504. I recall one student who had a tough time focusing on his work. His case manager came up with an idea of having two working spaces in the classroom—one was his work area and the other a free choice area. He was given a certain amount of time in each, which worked well in helping him focus when it was time to complete assignments.
- Remember that your room's appearance speaks to your beliefs about inclusivity. Do you have pictures and posters that are representative of all people? Are they all girls or all boys? All men or all women? Are the activities or words on posters or signs all gender specific ? I taught a course in world geography and cultures. Many of my posters were pictures of people from around the world. I had an LGBTQ+ rainbow sticker on the window of my doorway, which the diversity group had provided to alert students to LGBTQ+-friendly staff members. My subject matter lent itself to providing a more diverse outlook. If yours does not, consider adding visuals that convey your commitment to diversity.

It is difficult to embrace diversity of all kinds if you are not intentional, so plan to interact with students daily. If you do, you will enrich your life and the lives of your students.

What other ideas and strategies can you use to be inclusive?

Conclusion

If you have reached the end of this chapter, consider yourself a compassionate human being. It takes an open mind and open heart to consider implementing ways to reach students of all backgrounds and abilities. Young learners are fortunate to have you seeking and learning new ways to connect with them and to make their school days rich and meaningful. Uncovering the root of student actions or inactions can often prove revealing. If we know the needs of each student, we can support them in their efforts to gain a successful education.

We all want to be the teacher who is remembered because of a positive impact and not for any *negative* reasons. Being inclusive of all and building a robust TSR model through reflection and the willingness to change course if necessary is the vehicle to get there. Think of these concepts as the polish needed to keep you and your student stars shining brilliantly.

I hope the students' voices in this chapter have given you some pause. This may be an excellent time to process their perspectives.

Think of ways to help students with temporary or permanent disabilities, shyness, introversion, anxiety, trauma, low self-esteem, and who experience microaggressions or bullying. How can you prepare for teaching a sensitive curriculum while equipping yourself with measures to avoid and address disparaging terminology? What practices are helpful when altercations arise, and how can you interact with the administration if you disagree with how a situation was handled?

PART III

BUILD

Using a planned approach, you will learn more about your students' social, emotional, and academic needs and build a more positive, individualized learning environment where students feel secure, respected, and successful. Taking intentional time to reflect on your continued efforts to build a relationship with your students will take you far.

8

Design Your TSR Model

A goal without a plan is just a wish.
—Antoine de Saint-Exupéry

The first step in developing positive teacher-student relationships in the classroom is to plan individual conversation moments with each student. This may sound daunting but trust me, developing better relationships with them will be possible if you *plan* to get to know them. Planning is much better than winging it.

Although this chapter focuses on how to connect with students in a prescribed fashion, we cannot ignore the power of spontaneity found in impromptu interactions. Both formal and informal exchanges are valuable and contribute significantly to building teacher-student relationships. Some my argue that creating a plan is redundant, given the availability of nonverbal communication via email and district-approved social media methods. There is a problem with this type of thinking. Taking out face-to-face communication, at least initially, may not be the best method for creating strong bonds with students. An exception may be for shy students who choose not to communicate in person, at least initially. In the beginning, your teacher-student interaction needs to be more personal. You are attempting to build respect and trustworthiness. Communicating through technology alone can cause misunderstandings. At the very least, you want your students to know who you are and not take you the wrong way. Nothing can substitute for individual exchanges with each student.

In this chapter, you'll learn methods for creating a communication plan, preparing students for individual meetings, and keeping records of communications to ensure a foundation of teacher-student relationships and communication project planning.

Create a Communication Plan

Most teachers can build great relationships with their students but creating them with *all* students requires purposeful timing. It means setting and monitoring goals and being flexible to meet them. An organized plan ensures no child is left behind or slipping through the cracks. I realize the typical teaching day leaves little wiggle room for extras like a constructed time for personal student meetings. However, it is not the amount of time you take that counts; it is that you have taken the time. One or two minutes can be sufficient and powerful. I often used a minute or two to connect with students at the beginning of class, as they were packing up, during lunch, or at dismissal. Over a year, it made a difference with those I taught. These were incredibly productive moments for those who needed help, had behavioral issues, or seemed sullen or in need through observation. The optimum time to begin your TSR model design is when you receive your initial class list. However, you can start any time during the year. There is no need to get hung up on the date. The point is that you start. Begin by visualizing, establishing, and writing down when you will meet each student and set up a meeting goal for each day. That could be touching base with one student or a few students per day. Think about the time in your schedule that would work best. Perhaps it will be when other students are occupied, coming into class, getting ready, or working on an independent or collaborative activity. Next, think about how you will connect with each student. Will it be individually, in pairs, or in small focus groups? Will you meet with your students alphabetically, or by which ones appear to have the greatest need? Check your calendar for "black-out" dates, which might be days when you have an assembly, special presentation, or professional development. You may want to avoid the first week of school since there are so many interruptions and students are trying to transition to their new class environment. Once you have picked a date to begin, write the names of your students on the calendar date when you plan to meet with them. For a printable calendar for your use, please see the reproducible at the end of the chapter (page 136). Writing their names down will give you a better chance of completing your goal of meeting with them.

Your plan should be fluid, allowing for changes as needed. This gives you the best advantage in successfully creating teacher-student relationships. Substitute another student for any day a designated student may be absent, so you do not fall behind. Flexibility also means you can accommodate any student presenting themself in great need of your attention, which could be for behavioral, emotional, academic, or a host of other reasons. Just continue to move forward with your goal to meet with each student individually. Your impact will make a massive difference in the lives of your students.

You may think you have a plan in your head but consider the following advice. Having it in writing will guarantee you carry out your plans. In my experience and in witnessing other colleagues, best intentions seldom take flight unless written down.

Prepare Students for Meeting

Make students aware of your plan during the first week of school. Let them know that you plan to meet with each of them throughout the year to give them a *voice*, share joys or concerns, and get to know you. Tell them how and when you will meet and whether it will be in alphabetical or random order. I called it *talk time*, but you can come up with your own name and perhaps involve the students in selecting a name for your conversations. Your time is limited and valuable, yet powerful. Meeting with one student for even sixty seconds a day can help you make connections. Elementary teachers will most likely be able to meet with each student within a month. For secondary teachers, it will take longer. A solution for secondary teachers is to touch base with several students in one day, even if for time's sake, you meet as a group.

Make sure you give students an opt-out or alternative option such as email to communicate with you. Some students may not want to meet in person, and you certainly do not want them singled out because they are reluctant. They will come along once they feel comfortable. One way to make them feel less hesitant is to offer a sign-up for meeting times to the whole class. Post a calendar and have students fill in their names with the day they choose to meet with you. When students buy into something, they are likelier to go along with your initiatives. In my experience, only a handful of students preferred speaking with me solely via email or my school's internet-based platform. These consisted of a couple with much anxiety and a few others whose communication was affected by their learning disability. Most seemed to enjoy the personal interaction and attention. However, you may experience the complete opposite and a majority of students may wish to communicate via email or a hybrid of in-person and electronically. I noticed that our initial meetings opened the door for chats on the district learning management service called *Schoology* (https://apps.apple.com/us/app/schoology/id411766326). It made students feel more comfortable when they had questions or comments about what they were learning, their grades, or general insights. Managing my communication with my students was much easier and more frequent once students understood and were comfortable using Schoology. If you feel overwhelmed, I understand. However, with intentional communication plans, you can build teacher-student relationships and save time. You will be more knowledgeable of your students' personalities and capabilities. This way, you will circumvent the guessing about their social, emotional, and academic needs. A calculated plan for conversation moments is a time-saver rather than a burden.

Keep Records of Interactions

As you meet with students, writing brief notes can keep you organized and help you remember points to use in future conversations. Any method is fine, whether a journal, address book, binder with alphabetic tabs, spreadsheet, or notepad with a page for each student. I like the pen-and-paper method. A few years ago, I met a teacher who used an address book where she wrote comments under the letter corresponding to each student's last name. She made it a habit to jot down pertinent information about her students. I took this idea and found it easy to scribe notes about conversations with my students and their unique needs. Knowing our exchanges would be ongoing, the notes were helpful. It is old school, but I did not have to worry about the internet going down or losing everything. Sometimes, a template is useful for logging information when you meet with students. You can use the following example in figure 8.1 for your template.

Since we often have many students, taking notes makes life much easier and more productive in our ongoing quest to develop harmonious relationships. Use what is comfortable and logical for you. Personalize how you capture moments with your students and make them work to your advantage.

Interaction Record

Student Name: ______________________ Birthday: ______________

Character: ____

Family: ____

Hobbies & Interests: ______________________________________

Likes: ____

Dislikes: ____

Friends: ____

Areas of Strength: ____

____

Areas of Improvement: _____________________________________

____

Personal Goals & Other ____________________________________

____

____

____

Figure 8.1: Interaction record.

Instructions for Planning Your Communication

These suggested instructions are intended to give you some ideas for planning what I call your communication project or the facilitation piece in building teacher-student bonds. Use the space following this list to begin planning.

- Select a resource for note-taking (such as figure 8.1).
- Designate a page or two for each student and title the page with their name.
- Log any background information you already know about your students.
- Create a chronological meeting order.
- Write student names on a calendar showing when you will meet with them.
- Make your students aware of your plan.
- Plan. Meet. Repeat.

How and when will you schedule time to meet with your students?

Meet With Students

When you meet with each student the first time, reiterate the purpose of your chat. Reinforce your goal of learning more about them and why you feel it is a good idea. Go with their thoughts or guide them into conversation with prepared questions. Some of us need to prepare more than others who can let conversations grow organically. It is sensible to have some starter questions to make your meeting flow in either case. Know that you should not go down the list as if you are interviewing your student. This may come across as robotic and cold. Use one question to create a back and forth of conversation. Offer open-ended questions to avoid a dead-end yes or no response.

Pose questions such as, "What do you do for fun outside school?" Once your student responds, try to connect *personally* to the response. You will need to open up at this point. That is not always easy for some of us to do. If the student says they love to play softball, you could reply, "What position do you normally play?" Also, infuse your exchange with snippets about you. Add something like, "I've always enjoyed watching my sister's softball games," or you could volunteer the name of your favorite baseball team. Students are curious creatures and may enjoy hearing a little about you too.

That personal connection to a young life makes the difference between you and an unapproachable teacher. It helps to build teacher-student relationships, which is the goal.

Sometimes, one question may not be enough to spur a decent conversation, so you may need to engage further. Some students are shy, and we know they may not be forthcoming in chatting with you. That is to be expected. These students may need multiple questions, and you may feel like you are in an interview with them. To avoid this, share stories about you and let your personal side pour through. Watch as they begin to open up throughout the year. Setting the foundation with these students is essential. You need to know them and their learning style to reach and teach them. Finally, make sure you communicate that you are always there for them. Stating that you are available for face-to-face, written notes, or email communication is helpful to all students, especially those on the shy side. Reiterate your availability often.

To be prepared, look at the question suggestions on the following pages. Having a few favorite questions will prepare you for your student meeting time.

Conversation Starters

When meeting with younger students, start with questions or statements that may be easier to answer. Asking about their favorite things can help them to open up. I used the following starters at the beginning of the year to get to know students, and they have been helpful. The only exception was when I had a student who was shy, introverted, exhibited anxiety, or had a disability precluding them from interacting with me. Writing handwritten notes to them hoping they will reciprocate or using email and other district-approved platforms as mentioned before, may be helpful. However, if these methods do not work, stop or scale back on trying to communicate and seek assistance from the parents or guardians, counselor, or administrators.

- What is your favorite summer memory?
- Give me some clues about your favorite pet or a pet you would like to have.
- If you could stay in one subject for the entire day at school, what would it be and why?
- Tell me about your favorite thing to do when you are not in school.
- What is the funniest thing you ever heard or did?
- Describe a game you enjoy.
- What is your favorite birthday moment?
- What would you change at school if you were allowed?
- What is your superpower?

As students age, you can move on to more complex questioning or discussion prompts. It is common knowledge that secondary students can sometimes struggle with growing pains, and we may need to dig deeper into their feelings and learn more about them. In the following examples, the first list is designed to elicit an emotional response and was adapted from an article called, "Important Questions to Ask Your Students" (Elias, 2018). The second list consists of questions with a more neutral tone and are not designed to trigger an emotion. When using any of these suggestions, you may have to follow up with some explanation for students if they need help comprehending what you are asking. I also recommend sharing these inquiries with your counselor, who may shed some insight for their use in the classroom. The following are examples of emotive questions (designed to elicit an emotional response).

- When you are at school, what makes you feel accepted?
- In what situations do you feel that your voice is valued and given the consideration it deserves?
- In what situations do you feel most confident?
- Do you find yourself to be a follower, leader, or observer and why?
- What does your safe space look like?
- What does a safe and supportive environment look like to you?
- How do you handle disagreements or conflicts?
- What fears or anxieties do you think might hinder your academic or personal growth?
- Are there any challenges you have faced that you feel comfortable sharing?

The following are unemotive questions (designed as neutral, without intentionally triggering emotion).

- What dreams or goals do you have for your future path?
- Who do you rely on most and why?
- If you could change anything in your life now, what would it be?
- What is your special skill? Describe it.
- In what ways do you feel social media helps you to learn?
- What are your favorite hobbies or extracurricular activities?
- What books, movies, or TV shows do you enjoy?
- Are you more comfortable with visual, auditory, or hands-on type learning?
- How do you like group work or collaborative projects?
- Have you participated in any community service or volunteer work?

When your meeting concludes, hand students each a sticky note, have them put their name or initials on it, and ask them to keep it in their binder. At any time, they can use the note to write any questions they are uncomfortable asking you in person and then place the note on your desk.

Create a list of other questions you might ask your students during your meeting times with them.

Confidentiality

Although it is common sense, please keep your conversation with each student confidential. Do not share something you have learned about them unless you have permission. The only exception is if they share something with you that is life-threatening. As mentioned before, all fifty states require mandated reporting where a teacher is legally required to report child abuse (Child Welfare Information Gateway, 2023). For sensitive subjects that may arise, enlist the help of counselors, social workers, nurses, or administrators, provided you have these resources available in your district. When you are careful with your interactions, you will gain more respect from your students.

In understanding student privacy, we need to examine the law. Under FERPA (Family Educational Rights and Privacy Act), educational records can be requested by parents and guardians or for legal purposes. The bottom line is that any personal notes you create about a student are considered an "educational record" *unless* you are the only one using the information and *never* share it, written or verbally, with anyone else. This includes showing any personal student information in writing or discussing it with someone else. According to FERPA:

> Records which are kept in the sole possession of the maker of the records, are used only as a personal memory aid, and are not accessible or revealed to any other person except a temporary substitute for the maker of the records. (Protecting Student Privacy, n.d.)

Taking precautionary measures is a sound approach. Stick to the facts about students as you record notes and leave out any opinions or sensitive information.

What do you do when the school year ends, and you no longer have any need for your anecdotal notes or records? State laws vary, so check to see what your state requirements are for maintaining records or for disposal and coordinate with your school district too. Remember that in addition to hard copies of student documents, there is hard drive storage and the internet with emails and the cloud.

Encourage Communication

Projecting yourself as friendly has its advantages, especially when it comes to communication. You demonstrate that you are open to any concerns students may have. Creating an open-door policy and reinforce it by reminding students of its importance is another positive step in making them feel comfortable interacting with you (see figure 8.2, page 133). The following points can quickly and informally create an open communication atmosphere.

- Greet each student at the door every day.
- Have a box in the classroom where students can submit notes to you.
- Write a special sticky note for each student to ask you questions in writing.
- Schedule "How am I doing?" check-ins.
- Use personal conferencing about tests, quizzes, and projects.
- Ask an administrator to casually recognize a student for positive behavior or academic accomplishment.

- Use humor in the classroom.
- Show your humility.
- Use an in-district technological platform.
- Open up about yourself—be real.
- Create a community of learners and always reinforce respect.

What other ideas do you have to communicate and establish a rock-solid relationship with each student equitably? Make a list of your ideas.

Spur-of-the-Moment Communication

Student Name	Greeting	Follow-Up	Fist Bump	Compliment or Kind Word	Homework Check	Make-Up Work	Problem or Issue	Home Connection	Hobby or Sport Connection	Other
John										
Susie										
Julio										
Gwen										
Sven										
Lila										
Mark										
Jane										
Rahil										
Sensa										
Chan										
Han										
Jose										
Kev										

Figure 8.2: Documenting spur-of-the-moment communication.

Perpetuate Teacher-Student Relationships

You will want to continue building your relationship before, during, and after meeting with each student. This second tier of communication is when short exchanges occur outside your planned talk time. Let students know that the planned conversation moments do not preclude you from being available for any concerns or interaction with them each day. This is critically important. You want to create an open-door atmosphere, free from rigidity. I suggest modifying the impromptu chart to make it your own (see figure 8.2, page 133). Each day place a checkmark next to any student you speak with, even if it's just a hello or a few words about the latest football game. Check your list frequently for those individuals who have not interacted with you. This will be informative because you will see any missed connections you may have had with your students.

The everyday exchanges with your students are the sprinkles on the cake of your yearlong communication meeting plan. Continue to have conversation moments, talk time, or whatever you wish to name planned meetings with students throughout the year.

Conclusion

Your communication plan aims to set the foundation for building connections. It should be fluid, not rigid, and organized so you can learn about each student and form an exceptional relationship as much as possible. Visualize how you will meet initially. Will students prefer in-person, email, or a combination of the two? Do you anticipate needing any help from the counselor or parents to facilitate conversations with all your students? What will be your choice for recordkeeping? Information about your interactions will help you build on them as you circle back for subsequent meetings with your learners.

When you meet, use the provided conversation starters in this chapter or the ones you create. Make sure to tailor them to the specific age group you teach. When you hear their responses, remember they are confidential. Student privacy is a must. You will be building trust by using discretion.

Finally, one of the most impactful strategies I have found is logging spontaneous exchanges. It shows which students receive less teacher-student interaction over time and who needs more connection with you.

Designing a consistent communication plan is a simple idea with big rewards. It can be uplifting to know you are building equitable connections where students feel valued with a sense of belonging and realize opportunities for tremendous success.

Student Meeting Planning Calendar

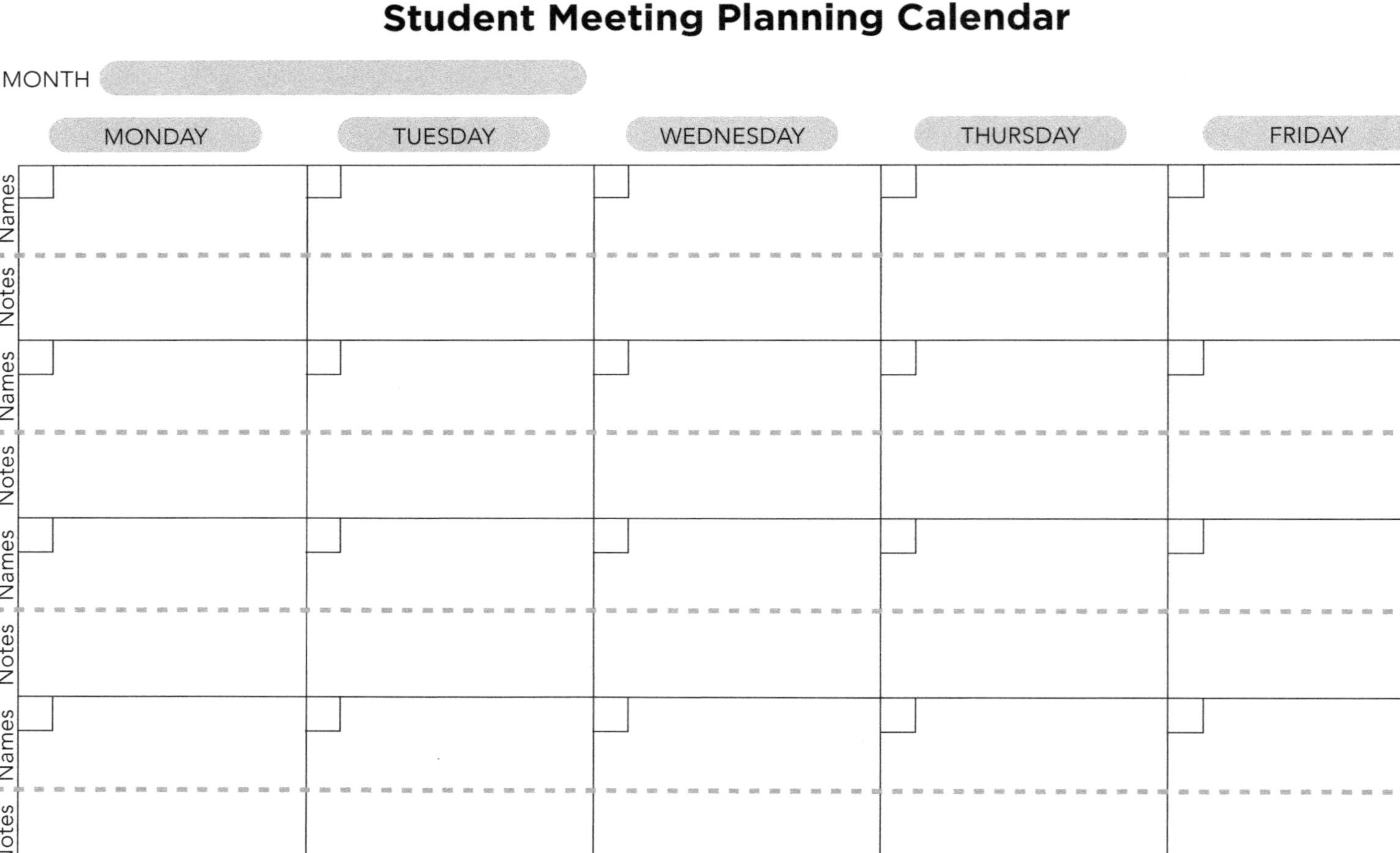

EPILOGUE

Your Reflections for Self-Efficacy and Change

Without reflection, we go blindly on our way, creating more unintended consequences, and failing to achieve anything useful.
—Margaret J. Wheatley

The TSR model is a framework that aims to guide you through all the necessary considerations for building meaningful connections. First, we must understand who we are as educators and people. What nonverbal signals do we project? How do students perceive us when we speak? Does what we say match what we do? From the first moment you meet your students, they form opinions of you. They are seeking your identity. They inspect your unique characteristics, the learning environment, how you instruct, and your discipline technique. Those first moments are when your brand emerges. It may be challenging to forge ties if they see inconsistencies or hypocrisies. Paying attention to your brand and what it reflects will guide students' perceptions and ultimately mold your reputation and your exchanges with them and other students.

As you continue showing more attributes through day-to-day activities and lessons, students begin to assess your communication and teaching style and whether you foster personalized learning, cooperative opportunities, and engagement. Students may start to feel growing positivity. They may also see you as a genuine and compassionate teacher who has crafted a remarkable village of learners—with an overflowing display of inclusivity and one that is void of discrimination. During the process, bonding takes hold, where students feel valued and respected, with a true sense of belonging because *you* made it happen.

How you get there is crucial. It can only come to fruition with your effort and planning. This next step is called the *building* concept of the TSR model. Designing and implementing an authentic communication plan is indispensable in connecting with students.

The key to forming and enhancing teacher-student relationships is to reflect, learn, and adapt to change. An ideal way to do this is through the process of observing and keeping notes about obstacles, social-emotional clues, behavioral issues, and other factors that might keep students from reaching their potential. Ongoing reflection and recording will allow you to build on your relationship foundations and steer students in the right direction for success.

Early in my career, as part of our district's evaluation system, I created a portfolio for self-evaluation that included the domains of planning, preparation, classroom environment, instruction, and professional responsibilities. I kept a weekly diary, recording my lessons, instruction experiences, student achievements and struggles, and interactions with students. As I reflected, I maintained a list of things that worked and things that did not work. I also involved the students by harnessing their input each week, which was a valuable tool for getting to know them better academically and personally. Through the process, I saw positive changes in my relationships with students, the quality of my instruction, my ability to manage behavior, and the likelihood of student success. Because it was such a powerful experience, in subsequent years, I continued to take anecdotal notes, improve where I was able, and as a result, forge better teacher-student relationships.

Even though a reflection and change approach has worked for me, I realize it may not be the same for others. *The Mirage*, a comprehensive study on teacher professional development, showed that one size does not fit all when it comes to improvement:

> Our research suggests that getting better at teaching is a lot like getting into better physical shape: a task that is difficult, highly individualized, and resistant to shortcuts. Just as there is no single diet and exercise plan that will work for everyone, it's all but certain that there is no single development experience or activity that will get results for every teacher. (TNTP, 2015, p. 34)

Our minds must be continually open to alternative ways to nurture teacher-student relationships. Through active personal reflection, we can sift and sort the necessary from the unnecessary. What is successful for us may not be successful for someone else. We must be willing to implement trial-and-error strategies and allow ourselves flexibility for change when needed. Permit yourself to accept when your way of doing things does not work. It is OK to be on the wrong track as long as you know when to hop off.

Regardless of your approach, however, I suggest you cannot enter a school year willy-nilly, thinking you can remember everything about a student during the relationship-building process. Recording your reflections is necessary for creating and maintaining close ties with students and for collaborative discourse with colleagues and even students' families. You need reflection-type data for improvement from year to year too. Reflect or record, refine or redefine what is necessary to build phenomenal connections with your students, and learn from your mistakes as you help students be the shining stars they are destined to be.

The profound impact of our words and actions underscores the significance of nurturing positive emotions and enduring relationships among our students. Never underestimate your worth and the effect on each student who crosses your path. They need you *to see* and *to be* there for them. I have often thought of it this way—we could be the only person who cares enough to build a rapport with them. The phrase inspires me to do more. The rewards of a systematic method of establishing bonds are immeasurable. When we make conscious connections, barriers shatter, learning takes flight, and beautiful lifelong memories become forever etched.

References and Resources

Allen, K.-A., Kern, M. L., Rozek, C. S., McInerney, D. M., & Slavich, G. M. (2021). Belonging: A review of conceptual issues, an integrative framework, and directions for future research. *Australian Journal of Psychology, 73*(1), 87–102. https://doi.org/10.1080/00049530.2021.1883409

Altamimi, A. , Shaman, F., & Alruban, A. (2020) A message length verification of modern messaging systems. *Journal of Computer and Communications, 8*, 103–113. https://doi.org/10.4236/jcc.2020.83010

Anderson, D., Stuart, M., Abadi, M., & Gal, S. (2019, January 5). *5 everyday hand gestures that can get you in serious trouble outside the US.* Accessed at www.businessinsider.com/hand-gestures-offensive-different-countries-2018-6 on January 9, 2024.

Anderson, J. (2019, November 20). *Unconscious bias in schools.* Accessed at www.gse.harvard.edu/news/19/11/harvard-edcast-unconscious-bias-schools on January 9, 2024.

Anderson, J. (2022, February 23). *The state of critical race theory in education.* Accessed at www.gse.harvard.edu/news/22/02/harvard-edcast-state-critical-race-theory-education on January 9, 2024.

Andersen, P. A. (2016). Eye behavior. In C. R. Berger & M. E. Roloff (Eds.), *The international encyclopedia of interpersonal communication.* Malden, MA: Wiley. https://doi.org/10.1002/9781118540190.wbeic152

Anti-Defamation League. (n.d.). *What we do.* Accessed at www.adl.org/about/education on January 9, 2024.

Aviles, C. (2018, March 30). *Being "the guide on the side" is not enough.* Accessed at https://techedupteacher.com/being-the-guide-on-the-side-is-not-enough-become-the-coo on March 27, 2024.

Banks, A. (2022, June 16). *Why social-emotional learning is important in special education* [Blog post]. Accessed at https://insightstobehavior.com/blog/social-emotional-learning-important-special-education on January 9, 2024.

Barni, D., Danioni, F., & Benevene, P. (2019). Teachers' self-efficacy: The role of personal values and motivations for teaching. *Frontiers in Psychology, 10.* https://doi.org/10.3389/fpsyg.2019.01645

Baumeister, R. F., & Leary, M. R. (1995). The need to belong: Desire for interpersonal attachments as a fundamental human motivation. *Psychological Bulletin, 117*(3), 497–529. https://doi.org/10.1037/0033-2909.117.3.497

Belsha, K., Barnum, M., & Aldrich, M. W. (2021, December 17). *Not getting into it: How critical race theory laws are cutting short classroom conversations.* Accessed at www.chalkbeat.org/2021/12/17/22840317/crt-laws-classroom-discussion-racism on January 9, 2024.

Belsky, G. (n.d.). *What is executive function?* Accessed at www.understood.org/en/articles/what-is-executive-function on January 9, 2024.

Benson, T. A., & Fiarman, S. E. (2019). *Unconscious bias in schools: A developmental approach to exploring race and racism.* Cambridge, MA: Harvard Education Press.

Bergin, C., & Bergin, D. (2009, May 21). Attachment in the classroom. Educational Psychology Review, 21(2), 141–170. https://doi.org/10.1007/s10648-009-9104-0

Black, R. (2020, December 1). *The gender identity terms you need to know.* Accessed at www.psycom.net/gender-identity-terms on January 9, 2024.

Bosch, O. J., & Young, L. J. (2017). Oxytocin and social relationships: From attachment to bond disruption. *Behavioral Pharmacology of Neuropeptides: Oxytocin, 35*, 97–117. https://doi.org/10.1007/7854_2017_10

Bowman, J. D. (2020, August 14). *Creating a schoolwide racial and social justice initiative.* Accessed at www.edutopia.org/article/creating-schoolwide-racial-and-social-justice-initiative on January 9, 2024.

Bowman, J. M., & Compton, B. L. (2022). Interpersonal oculesics: Eye-related signals of attraction, interest, and connection. In R. J. Sternberg & A. Kostic (Eds.), *Nonverbal communication in close relationships: What words don't tell us* (pp. 1–23). Cham, Switzerland: Palgrave Macmillan.

Bowden, M. (2013, October 28). Body language expert keynote Mark Bowden at Tedx Toronto: The importance of being inauthentic [Video file]. Accessed at https://youtube.com/watch?v=rk_SMBIW1mg on March 27, 2024.

Branstetter, R. (2020, October 9). *How teachers can help students with special needs navigate distance learning.* Accessed at https://greatergood.berkeley.edu/article/item/how_teachers_can_help_students_with_special_needs_navigate_distance_learning on January 9, 2024.

Breiseth, L., Garcia, S., & Butler, S. (n.d.). *How to use culturally responsive teaching in the classroom.* Accessed at https://www.understood.org/en/articles/how-to-use-culturally-responsive-teaching-in-the-classroom on March 21, 2024.

Brooks, D. (2021, July 22). *How racist is America?* Accessed at www.nytimes.com/2021/07/22/opinion/how-racist-is-america.html on January 9, 2024.

Bruner, J. (1983). *In search of mind.* New York: Harper & Row.

CHARACTER COUNTS! (2020). *About CHARACTER COUNTS!* Accessed at https://charactercounts.org/history on January 9, 2024.

Chastain, J. (Host). (2018a, October 8). #81 lead meaningful race conversations with Matthew Kay pt.1 [Audio podcast episode]. In *Teach me, Teacher.* Accessed at https://teachmeteacherpodcast.com/2018/10/08/81-lead-meaningful-race-conversations-with-matthew-kay-pt-1 on January 9, 2024.

Chastain, J. (Host). (2018b, October 15). #82 lead meaningful race conversations with Matthew Kay pt.2. In *Teach me, Teacher.* Accessed at https://teachmeteacherpodcast.com/2018/10/15/82-not-light-but-fire-with-matthew-kay-pt-2 on January 9, 2024.

Child Welfare Information Gateway. (2019). *Penalties for failure to report and false reporting of child abuse and neglect.* Accessed at https://cwig-prod-prod-drupal-s3fs-us-east-1.s3.amazonaws.com/public/documents/report.pdf?VersionId=L5R7xLMqtiiYYGz3jjpHmCkeIIr3ve9K on January 9, 2024.

Child Welfare Information Gateway. (2023). *Immunity for persons who report child abuse and neglect.* Accessed at https://cwig-prod-prod-drupal-s3fs-us-east-1.s3.amazonaws.com/public/documents/reporterimmunity.pdf?VersionId=k3Maq6sbYS4VRNwBTMjFPMxMUntES6Er on January 9, 2024.

Chung, S., & Son, J.-W. (2020). *Visual perception in autism spectrum disorder: A review of neuroimaging studies. Soa Chongsonyon Chongsin Uihak, 31*(3), 105–120.

Cuncic, A. (2023, March 28). *How to read facial expressions.* Accessed at https://verywellmind.com/understanding-emotions-through-facial-expressions-3024851#How%20to%20Identify%20Facial%20Expressions%20by%20Facial%20Feature on March 27, 2024.

Danon, C. (2019, August 16). *French body talk: 20 fun gestures for fluency without words* [Blog post]. Accessed at https://frenchpod101.com/blog/2019/08/16/french-body-gestures/#Positive%20Gestures on March 28, 2024..

Demarais, A., & White, V. (2004). *First impressions: What you don't know about how others see you.* New York: Random House.

Derek Bok Center for Teaching and Learning. (2003, September 2). *Encouraging students in a racially diverse classroom.* Accessed at www.butte.edu/diversity/documents/pdfs/diversity/teaching/Teaching%20tips%20race%20in%20the%20classroom.PDF on January 10, 2024.

Dunbar, N. E., & Segrin, C. (2012). *Clothing and teacher credibility: An application of expectancy violations theory.* International Scholarly Research Notices, 140517.

Dyches, T. T., Carter, N. J., & Prater, M. A. (2012). *A teacher's guide to communicating with parents: Practical strategies for developing successful relationships.* Upper Saddle River, NJ: Pearson Education.

The Editorial Team. (2020, June 8). *Why should you not use all capital letters in an email?* Accessed at www.womleadmag.com/why-should-you-not-use-all-capital-letters-in-an-email on January 10, 2024.

Elias, M. J. (2018, July 30). *Important questions to ask your students.* Accessed at www.edutopia.org/article/important-questions-ask-your-students on January 9, 2024.

Faderman, L. (2015). *The gay revolution: The story of the struggle.* New York: Simon & Schuster.

Farhah, I., Saleh, A. Y., & Safitri, S. (2021). The role of student-teacher relationship to teacher subjective well-being as moderated by teaching experience. *Journal of Education and Learning, 15*(2), 267–274. https://doi.org/10.11591/edulearn.v15i2.18330

Folk, J. (2021, May 19). *Pupils anxiety symptoms—dilated or contracted.* Accessed at www.anxietycentre.com/anxiety-disorders/symptoms/pupils-anxiety-symptoms on January 9, 2024.

Freire, P. (2000). *Pedagogy of the oppressed* (30th anniversary ed.; M. B. Ramos, Trans.). New York: Continuum. (Original work published 1968)

Frey, W. H. (2020, July 1). *The nation is diversifying even faster than predicted, according to new census data.* Accessed at www.brookings.edu/articles/new-census-data-shows-the-nation-is-diversifying-even-faster-than-predicted on January 9, 2024.

Furrer, C., & Skinner, E. (2003). Sense of relatedness as a factor in children's academic engagement and performance. Journal of Educational Psychology, 95(1), 148–162. Accessed at https://psycnet.apa.org/doiLanding?doi=10.1037%2F0022-0663.95.1.148 on March 28, 2024.

Gardner, H. (2011). *Frames of mind: The theory of multiple intelligences.* New York: Basic Books.

Gollwitzer, P. M. (1999). Implementation intentions: Strong effects of simple plans. *American Psychologist, 54*(7), 493–503. https://doi.org/10.1037/0003-066X.54.7.493

Grzybowski, A., & Kupidura-Majewski, K. (2019). What is color and how it is perceived? *Clinics in Dermatology, 37*(5), 392–401.

Hartwell-Walker, M. (2016, May 17). *Why friends disappear when crisis turns chronic.* Accessed at https://psychcentral.com/lib/why-friends-disappear-when-crisis-turns-chronic#1 on January 9, 2024.

Henry, T. (2016, January 7). *How the world's best public speakers find an authentic voice.* Accessed at www.inc.com/todd-henry/3-qualities-to-develop-an-authentic-voice.html on January 9, 2024.

Howlett, N., Pine, K., Orakçioglu, I., & Fletcher, B. (2013, February 22). The influence of clothing on first impressions. Rapid and positive responses to minor changes in male attire. Journal of Fashion Marketing and Management, 17(1), 38–48. https://doi.org/10.1108/13612021311305128

Hughes, J. (Director). (1986). *Ferris Bueller's day off* [Film]. Hollywood, CA: Paramount Pictures.

Jones, C. (2022, March 29). *Parents' guide to 504 plans and IEPs: What they are and how they're different.* Accessed at https://edsource.org/2022/parents-guide-to-504-plans-and-ieps-what-they-are-and-how-theyre-different/669493 on January 9, 2024.

Jones, S. M., & Kahn, J. (2017, September 13). *The evidence base for how we learn: Supporting students' social, emotional, and academic development.* Washington, DC: Aspen Institute. Accessed at www.aspeninstitute.org/wp-content/uploads/2018/03/FINAL_CDS-Evidence-Base.pdf on January 9, 2024.

Josephson, M. (1992). Eight sentences that changed the world: The Aspen Declaration [Blog post]. Accessed at https://whatwillmatter.com/2013/10/eight-sentences-that-changed-the-world-the-aspen-declaration on March 28, 2024.

Josephson, M. (2023), *Critical education outcomes: Josephson Institute Model Standards for Academic, Social, Emotional, and Character Development and School Culture.* Des Moines, IA: Ray Center at Drake University. Accessed at https://charactercounts.org/wp-content/uploads/2023/08/Model-Standards-2023.pdf on March 28, 2024.

Kay, M. R. (2018). *Not light, but fire: How to lead meaningful race conversations in the classroom.* Portland, ME: Stenhouse.

Kendi, I. X. (2019). *How to be an antiracist.* New York: One World.

Kendi, I. X. (2023). *Stamped from the beginning: A graphic history of racist ideas in America* (J. C. Gill, Illus.). New York: Random House.

Kosciw, J. G., Clark, C. M., & Menard, L. (2022). *The 2021 National School Climate Survey.* New York: GLSEN. Accessed at www.glsen.org/sites/default/files/2022-10/NSCS-2021-Full-Report.pdf on January 9, 2024.

Kraft, M. A., & Dougherty, S. M. (2013). The effect of teacher–family communication on student engagement: Evidence from a randomized field experiment. *Journal of Research on Educational Effectiveness, 6*(3), 199–222.

Lightner, L. (n.d.). *40 IEP goals for reading comprehension, including strategies.* Accessed at https://adayinourshoes.com/reading-comprehension-strategies on January 9, 2024.

Lynch, M. (2016, March 19). *4 ways to help your students embrace diversity.* Accessed at www.theedadvocate.org/4-ways-to-help-your-students-embrace-diversity on January 9, 2024.

Mason, C., Ross, R., Harris, O., & Flanders, J. (2024). *Little learner, big hearts: A teacher's guide to nurturing empathy and equity in early childhood.* Bloomington, IN: Solution Tree Press.

Mayo, C. (2022). *LGBTQ youth and education: Policies and practices* (2nd ed.). New York: Teachers College Press.

Menakem, R. (2017). *My grandmother's hands: Racialized trauma and the pathway to mending our hearts and bodies.* Las Vegas, NV: Central Recovery Press.

Mental Health First Aid USA. (2019, August 15). *Five tips for nonjudgmental listening.* Accessed at www.mentalhealthfirstaid.org/2019/08/five-tips-for-nonjudgmental-listening on January 9, 2024.

Meyer, E. J. (2009). *Gender, bullying, and harassment: Strategies to end sexism and homophobia in schools.* New York: Teachers College Press.

Microaggression. (n.d.). *In Merriam-Webster's online dictionary.* Accessed at www.merriam-webster.com/dictionary/microaggression on January 8, 2024.

National Center for Education Statistics. (2023). *Characteristics of public school teachers.* Accessed at https://nces.ed.gov/programs/coe/pdf/2023/clr_508.pdf on January 9. 2024.

National Conference of State Legislatures. (2023, May 30). *Public records law and state legislatures.* Accessed at www.ncsl.org/cls/public-records-law-and-state-legislatures on January 10, 2024.

Navarro, J. (2018). *The dictionary of body language: A field guide to human behavior.* New York: HarperCollins.

Navarro, R. (n.d.). *Unconscious bias training: About unconscious bias* [Video file]. Accessed at https://diversity.ucsf.edu/programs-resources/training/unconscious-bias-training on March 21, 2024.

Ni, P. (2021, November 2). *What are overt and covert types of racism?* [Blog post]. Accessed at www.psychologytoday.com/gb/blog/communication-success/202111/what-are-overt-and-covert-types-of-racism on January 9, 2024.

Okonofua, J. A., Paunesku, D., & Walton, G. M. (2016). Brief intervention to encourage empathic discipline cuts suspension rates in half among adolescents. *Proceedings of the National Academy of Sciences, 113*(19), 5221–5226. https://doi.org/10.1073/pnas.1523698113

Oster, M. (2019, September 25). *What does 'Jew down' mean, and why do people find it offensive?* Accessed at www.jta.org/2019/09/25/culture/what-does-jew-down-mean-and-why-do-people-find-it-offensive on January 9, 2024.

Parks-Stamm, E. J., & Gollwitzer, P. M. (2009). Goal implementation: The benefits and costs of if-then planning. In G. B. Moskowitz & H. Grant (Eds.), *The psychology of goals* (pp. 362–391). New York: Guilford Press.

Pease, A., & Pease, B. (2006). *The definitive book of body language.* New York: Bantam Books.

The President and Fellows of Harvard College. (2024). *Inclusive course design.* Derek Bok Center, Harvard University. Accessed at https://bokcenter.harvard.edu/inclusive-course-design on March 21, 2024.

Piaget, J., & Inhelder, B. (1969). *The psychology of the child.* New York: Basic Books.

Positive Action Staff. (2023, September 13). *Teaching strategies for students with special needs* [Blog post]. Accessed at www.positiveaction.net/blog/teaching-special-education-strategies on January 9, 2024.

The President and Fellows of Harvard College. (2024). Inclusive course design. Derek Bok Center, Harvard University. Accessed at https://bokcenter.harvard.edu/inclusive-course-design on March 21, 2024.

Prismic. (2019). *Easy steps to an inclusive classroom.* Accessed at https://www.genderspectrum.org/resources on April 16th, 2024.

Prochazka, J., Ovcari, M., & Durinik, M. (2020). Sandwich feedback: The empirical evidence of its effectiveness. *Learning and Motivation, 71,* 101649. https://doi.org/10.1016/j.lmot.2020.101649

Project READY. (n.d.). *Module 4: Implicit bias & microaggressions.* Accessed at https://ready.web.unc.edu/section-1-foundations/module-4-implicit-bias-microaggressions on January 8, 2024.

Protecting Student Privacy. (n.d.). *What records are exempted from FERPA?* Accessed at https://studentprivacy.ed.gov/faq/what-records-are-exempted-ferpa on January 10, 2024.

Racism. (n.d.a). In *Dictionary.com.* Accessed at www.dictionary.com/browse/racism?s=t on January 26, 2021.

Racism. (n.d.b). In *Merriam-Webster's online dictionary*. Accessed at www.merriam-webster.com/dictionary/racism on January 26, 2021.

Rakestraw, M. (2017, October 13). *8 resources for teaching about unconscious bias*. Accessed at https://humaneeducation.org/9-resources-teaching-unconscious-bias on January 10, 2024.

Ray Center at Drake University. (2020). The Aspen declaration & creation of CHARACTER COUNTS!® Accessed at https://charactercounts.org/wp-content/uploads/2019/02/Website-The-Aspen-Declaration-Final2.26.2019.pdf on April 11, 2024.

Reinius, H., Korhonen, T., & Hakkarainen, K. (2021). The design of learning spaces matters: Perceived impact of the deskless school on learning and teaching. *Learning Environments Research, 24*, 339–354. https://doi.org/10.1007/s10984-020-09345-8

Rodat, S. (2019). Listening in verbal communication: Aspects regarding active listening in theoretical models of social work. *Annals of the University of Craiova for Journalism, Communication and Management, 5*(1), 139–158.

Roorda, D. L., Jak, S., Zee, M., Oort, F. J., & Koomen, H. M. Y. (2017). Affective teacher–student relationships and students' engagement and achievement: A meta-analytic update and test of the mediating role of engagement. *School Psychology Review, 46*(3), 239–261. https://doi.org/10.17105/SPR-2017-0035.V46-3

Ryan, C. L., & Hermann-Wilmarth, J. M. (2018). *Reading the rainbow: LGBTQ-inclusive literacy instruction in the elementary classroom*. New York: Teachers College Press.

Salamondra, T. (2021). Effective communication in schools. *BU Journal of Graduate Studies in Education, 13*(1), 22–26.

Scroope, C. (2021). *Japanese culture: Communication*. Accessed at https://culturalatlas.sbs.com.au/japanese-culture/japanese-culture-communication#japanese-culture-communication on March 28. 2024.

Scroope, C., & Evason, N. (2017). *Do's and don'ts*. Accessed at https://culturalatlas.sbs.com.au/chinese-culture/chinese-culture-do-s-and-don-ts on March 27, 2024.

Senju, A., & Csibra, G. (2008). Gaze following in human infants depends on communicative signals. *Current Biology, 18*(9), 668–671. https://doi.org/10.1016/j.cub.2008.03.059

Senning, D. P. (2013). *Emily Post's manners in a digital world: Living well online*. New York: Open Road Integrated Media.

Sententiae Antiquae. (2017, May 27). *Head and heart: A quotation falsely attributed to Aristotle*. Accessed https://sententiaeantiquae.com/2017/05/27/head-and-heart-a-quotation-falsely-attributed-to-aristotle on March 28, 2024.

Shulman, R. D. (2019, December 26). *Why teachers need a personal brand and how to create one*. Accessed at www.forbes.com/sites/robynshulman/2019/12/26/why-teachers-need-a-personal-brand-and-how-to-create-one/?sh=189bde9b177c on January 10, 2024.

Simon Wiesenthal Center. (n.d.). *Teacher's guide and resources*. Accessed at www.museumoftolerance.com/for-professionals/programs-workshops/free-professional-development-for-educators/teachers-guide-and-resources on January 10, 2024.

Singleton, G. E. (2022). *Courageous conversations about race: A field guide for achieving equity in schools and beyond* (3rd ed.). Thousand Oaks, CA: Corwin Press.

Spataro, S. E., & Bloch, J. (2017). *"Can you repeat that?" Teaching active listening in management education*. Journal of Management Education, 42(2), 168–198. https://doi.org/10.1177/1052562917748696

Taylor, P. (2023, May 1). *What does angry body language look like (See the signs)*. Accessed at https://bodylanguagematters.com/angry-body-language on March 28, 2024.

TNTP. (2015). *The mirage: Confronting the hard truth about our quest for teacher development*. Accessed at https://tntp.org/wp-content/uploads/2023/02/TNTP-Mirage_2015.pdf on March 28, 2024..

Treasure, J. (2013, June). *How to speak so that people want to listen* [Video file]. Accessed at www.ted.com/talks/julian_treasure_how_to_speak_so_that_people_want_to_listen on January 10, 2024.

Tslpursky, G. (2020, July 13). *What is unconscious bias (and how you can defeat it)* [Blog post]. Accessed at www.psychologytoday.com/us/blog/intentional-insights/202007/what-is-unconscious-bias-and-how-you-can-defeat-it on January 10, 2024.

Turk, V. (2019). *Kill reply all: A modern guide to online etiquette, from social media to work to love*. New York: Plume.

The Understood Team. (n.d.). *Setting annual IEP goals: What you need to know*. Accessed at www.understood.org/en/articles/setting-annual-iep-goals-what-you-need-to-know on January 10, 2024.

UNESCO. (2020). *Global education monitoring report 2020: Inclusion and education—All means all*. Paris: Author. Accessed at https://unesdoc.unesco.org/ark:/48223/pf0000373718 on January 10, 2024.

University of Edinburgh. (2022, December 15). *Effects of microaggressions*. Accessed at www.ed.ac.uk/equality-diversity/students/microaggressions/effects-of-microaggressions on January 10, 2024.

U.S. Department of Education. (n.d.). *About IDEA*. Accessed at https://sites.ed.gov/idea/about-idea on January 10, 2024.

U.S. Department of Education. (2017, May 2). *Sec. 300.39 special education*. Accessed at https://sites.ed.gov/idea/regs/b/a/300.39 on January 10, 2024.

U.S. Department of Education. (2021, June). *Supporting transgender youth in school*. Accessed at www2.ed.gov/about/offices/list/ocr/docs/ed-factsheet-transgender-202106.pdf on January 10, 2024.

U.S. Department of Education. (2022a, January 12). *Disability discrimination*. Accessed at www2.ed.gov/about/offices/list/ocr/frontpage/pro-students/disability-pr.html on January 10, 2024.

U.S. Department of Education. (2022b, July 19). *Fact sheet.* Accessed at www2.ed.gov/about/offices/list/ocr/docs/504-discipline-factsheet.pdf on January 10, 2024.

U.S. Department of Education. (2023, June 21). *U.S. Department of Education toolkit: Creating inclusive and nondiscriminatory school environments for LGBTQI+ students.* Accessed at www2.ed.gov/about/offices/list/ocr/docs/lgbtqi-student-resources-toolkit-062023.pdf on December 9, 2023.

Van Edwards, V. (n.d.). *The definitive guide to reading microexpressions (facial expressions).* Accessed at www.scienceofpeople.com/microexpressions on January 9, 2024.

Vygotsky, L. S. (1978). *Mind in society: The development of higher psychological processes.* Cambridge, MA: Harvard University Press.

Walker, T. (2018, June 8). *Who is the average U.S. teacher?* Accessed at https://nea.org/advocating-for-change/new-from-nea/who-average-us-teacher on March 28, 2024.

We Are Teachers Staff. (2023, February 3). *What is a flipped classroom, and is it right for my students and me?* Accessed at www.weareteachers.com/what-is-a-flipped-classroom on January 10, 2024.

Wei, Z., Yan, Y., Huang, L., & Nie, J. (2017). Inferring intrinsic correlation between clothing style and wearers' personality. Multimedia Tools and Applications, 76(19), 20273–20285. https://doi.org/10.1007/s11042-017-4778-7

Willis, J., & Todorov, A. (2006). First impressions: Making up your mind after a 100-ms exposure to a face. Psychological Science, 17(7), 592–598.

Yoon, S., & Kim, Y.-K. (2022). Possible oxytocin-related biomarkers in anxiety and mood disorders. *Progress in Neuro-Psychopharmacology and Biological Psychiatry, 116,* 110531. https://doi.org/10.1016/j.pnpbp.2022.110531

Zemeckis, R. (Director). (2000). *Cast away* [Film]. Los Angeles: 20th Century Fox.

Zmuda, A., Curtis, G., & Ullman, D. (2015). *Learning personalized: The evolution of the contemporary classroom.* San Francisco: Jossey-Bass.

Index

C

Embracing Relational Teaching
Anthony R. Reibel
When you shift to relational pedagogy, you establish connections that help students feel valued, respected, and heard, which leads to enhanced student engagement. This book explores the relational approach and offers strategies to embed teacher-student relationships into everyday interactions and learning.
BKF949

I'm Listening
Beth Pandolpho
Rely on *I'm Listening* to help drive deeper, more meaningful learning by integrating relationship building into lesson design. Using the book's practical strategies will help you empower learners to succeed at all subjects by being proficient readers, writers, speakers, and listeners.
BKF926

Building Bridges
Don Parker
Research shows that discipline problems are one of the greatest challenges in education. In *Building Bridges*, author Don Parker shows educators how to address this issue head-on, to build teacher-student relationships and create a welcoming learning environment that promotes engagement and achievement.
BKF846

Power Engage
Carlos Johnson
Gain seven strategies designed to help you engage students and families by building performance-based relationships. Drawing from research and his own experiences as an education leader, Coach Carlos Johnson shares practical guidance on how to deepen the impact of your instruction.
BKG100

Solution Tree | Press

Visit SolutionTree.com or call 800.733.6786 to order.